I0559337

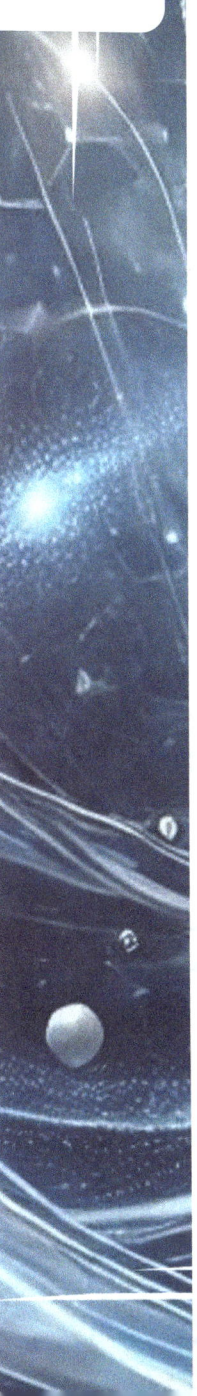

$\mathcal{B}$EYOND

TESLA: ADVANCING THE SCIENCE OF ENERGY HEALING

Dr. Constance Santego
Maximillian Enterprises
Kelowna, BC

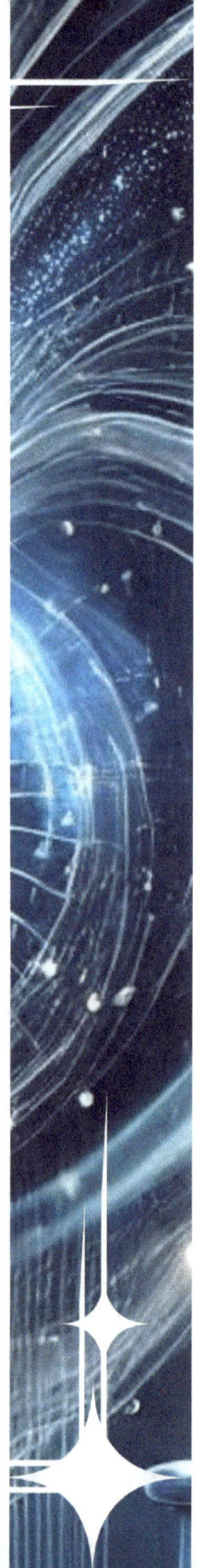

Beyond Tesla: Advancing The Science Of Energy Healing
Copyright © 2024 by Dr. Constance Santego.

Copy Editor & Interior Design: Dr. Constance Santego
Book Layout: ©2017 BookDesignTemplates.com
Ordering Information:
Quantity sales. Special discounts are available on quantity purchases by corporations, associations, and others. For details, contact the email below (addressed: "Special Sales Department").

Trade Paperback ISBN: 978-1-990062-43-8
eBook ISBN: 978-1-990062-44-5
Created and published In Canada. Printed and bound in the United States of America

First Edition
Published by Maximillian Enterprises
Kelowna, BC
Canada
www. maximilliane.com
staff@maximilliane.com

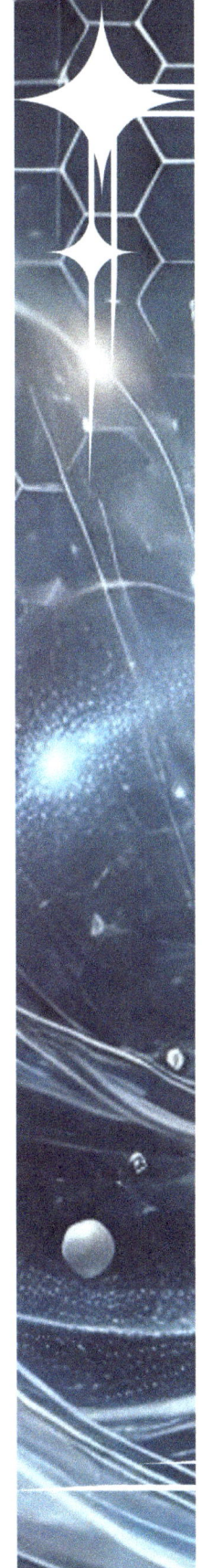

Dedicated to the pioneers of energy medicine, the visionary inventors and subtle energy healers who, following in Nikola Tesla's footsteps, have boldly expanded the frontiers of science and healing. Your relentless pursuit of innovation and understanding continues to illuminate the path toward a future where energy and medicine unite for the betterment of all.

"IF YOU WANT TO FIND THE SECRETS OF THE UNIVERSE, THINK IN TERMS OF ENERGY, FREQUENCY, AND VIBRATION."
—NIKOLA TESLA

ALSO BY DR. CONSTANCE SANTEGO

FICTION
The Nine Spiritual Gifts Series:
Journey of a Soul – (Vol 1 Michael)
Language of a Soul – (Vol 2 Gabriel)
Prophecy of a Soul – (Vol 3 Bath Kol)
Healing of a Soul – (Vol 4 Raphael)
Miracles of a Soul – (Vol 5 Hamied)
Knowledge of a Soul – (Vol 6 Raziel)

NONFICTION
The Intuitive Life, The Gift of Prophecy, Third Edition
Fairy Tales, Dreams and Reality… Where Are You On Your Path? Second Edition
Your Persona… The Mask You Wear
Angelic Lifestyle, A Vibrant Lifestyle
Angelic Lifestyle 42-Day Energy Cleanse
Archangel Michael's Soul Retrieval Guide
Tesla and the Future of Energy Medicine
Tesla's Code: *Mastering Energy, Frequency, and Creative Power*
Scaling Beyond 6 Figures: *Strategies for Health & Wellness Professionals*
Beyond the Mind: *Harnessing the Power of Astral Projection for Creative Awakening*
Bend, Don't Break: *Finding Your Way Back to Abundance*
Ring Therapy: *A Guide to Healing and Balance*
Ring Therapy Pocket Guide
Floraopathy™: *The Art and Science of Vibrational Healing with Essential Oils*

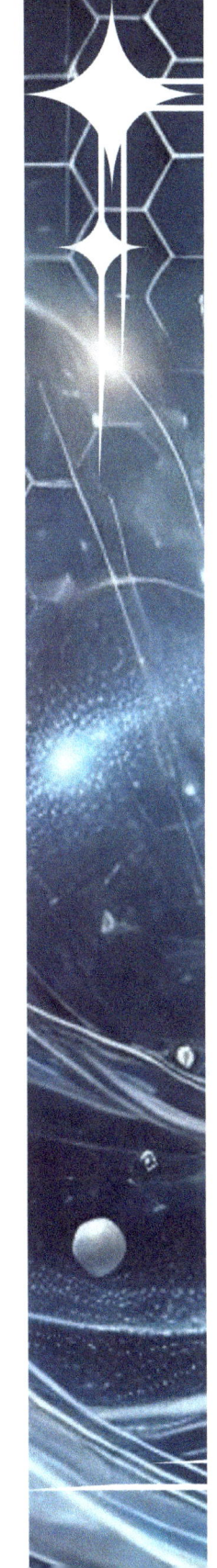

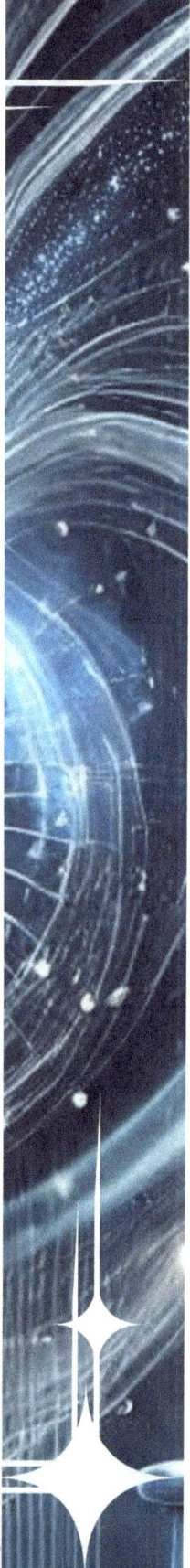

SECRETS OF A HEALER, SERIES:

Magic Of Aromatherapy (Vol I)
Magic Of Reflexology (Vol II)
Magic Of The Gifts (Vol III)
Magic Of Muscle Testing (Vol IV)
Magic Of Iridology (Vol V)
Magic Of Massage (Vol VI)
Magic Of Hypnotherapy (Vol VII)
Magic Of Reiki (Vol VIII)
Magic Of Advanced Aromatherapy (Vol IX)
Magic Of Esthetics (Vol X)
The Reiki Master's Manual (Vol XI)

ADULT COLORING JOURNALS

SERIES - ZEN COLORING:
Quantum Energy and Mindful Living Journal (Vol 1)
Reiki Energy Journal (Vol 2)
Nine Spiritual Gifts Journal (Vol 3)
I Forgive Journal (Vol 4)

SERIES – COLORING PROSPERITY:
Genie-Inspired Mandalas and Wealth Journal (Vol 1)
Entrepreneurial Mindset Reboot (Vol 2)

SERIES – HARMONIC MIND CODE:
Harmonic Mind Code Coloring Journal (Vol 1)

FOR CHILDREN

I am Big Tonight. I Don't Need the Light!

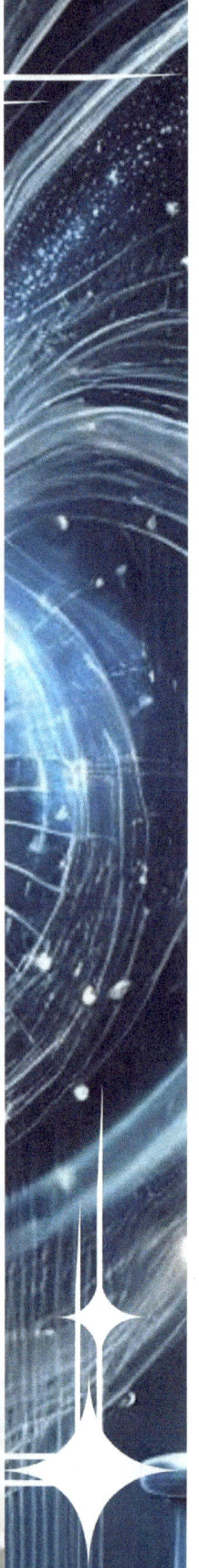

Contents

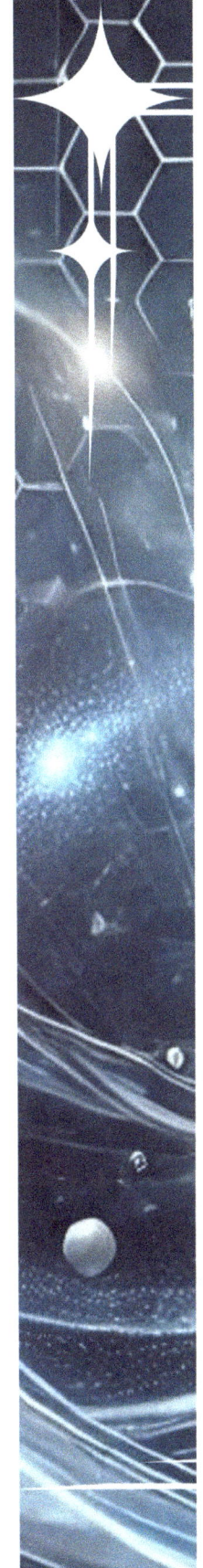

"MEDICINE REPAIRS THE BODY. HEALING AWAKENS THE SOUL. ENERGY MEDICINE DOES BOTH."
—RHYS THOMAS

Foreword

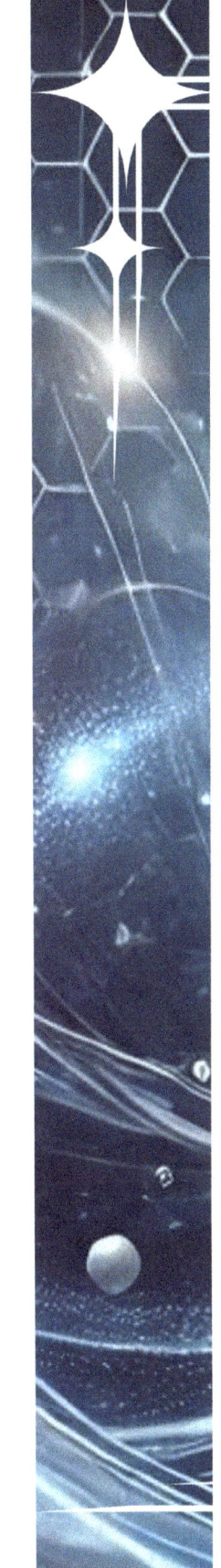

In ***Tesla and the Future of Energy Medicine (Book 1)***, we embarked on a journey to explore the profound connections between Nikola Tesla's groundbreaking work in electromagnetism and the emerging field of energy medicine. Tesla, whose contributions transformed the understanding of electricity and power, also held visionary insights that extended into the subtle, invisible forces shaping human health and healing. That initial exploration laid the foundation for a new perspective on how energy interacts with the human body, hinting at a future where healing is vibrational, energetic, and holistic.

*Beyond Tesla: **Advancing the Science of Energy Healing*** (Book 2) took this understanding further, bridging the gap between Tesla's pioneering theories and the rapidly evolving science of energy medicine today. In that volume, we delved deeper into concepts like quantum physics, biofield therapies, and vibrational healing, discovering how ancient wisdom is converging with cutting-edge technology. It is in this convergence that Tesla's vision finds new relevance, as his ideas continue to inspire and inform modern approaches to healing through energy, frequency, and vibration.

In ***Tesla's Code: Mastering Energy, Frequency, and Creative Power (Book 3)***, we move into the next phase of this exploration. Building on Tesla's legacy, this book provides practical tools and techniques for mastering the subtle energies that govern both our inner world and the universe around us. By examining the

principles of energy, frequency, and vibration through Tesla's lens, we unlock new pathways for healing, personal empowerment, and creative expression. *Tesla's Code* represents the culmination of Tesla's influence on energy healing, offering readers a comprehensive guide to applying these concepts in their own lives and practices.

As you engage with the ideas and practices in this book, we encourage you to open yourself to the transformative potential of energy medicine. Whether you are a healer, researcher, or someone seeking to deepen your understanding of Tesla's work, this book offers a roadmap for navigating the intricate relationship between energy and health. Together, we move beyond theory into the realm of practical application, where the mysteries of the universe can be harnessed for healing and transformation.

Preface

In *Tesla and the Future of Energy Medicine*, we embarked on a journey that connected Nikola Tesla's visionary insights with the emerging field of energy medicine. We explored how his groundbreaking work in electromagnetism laid the foundation for a new understanding of healing, one that encompasses not only the physical but also the vibrational and energetic aspects of health. That book served as an introduction, opening the door to a new era where the boundaries of traditional healthcare are expanded by incorporating the subtle, unseen forces that Tesla sought to harness.

With *Beyond Tesla: Advancing the Science of Energy Healing*, we now move further into this exploration. This book is not just a continuation—it is a deep dive into the next phase of energy medicine, where the science of healing is evolving at an unprecedented pace. As the world of healthcare transforms, we are witnessing a growing acceptance of concepts that were once considered esoteric, such as the biofield, frequency healing, and quantum consciousness. The convergence of ancient wisdom with modern technological advancements is revealing new pathways to health and wellness, pathways that Tesla himself may have only glimpsed in his visionary imagination.

Tesla once famously stated, "If you want to find the secrets of the universe, think in terms of energy, frequency, and vibration." This simple yet profound statement continues to inspire and inform the cutting-edge science behind energy healing. In this volume, we

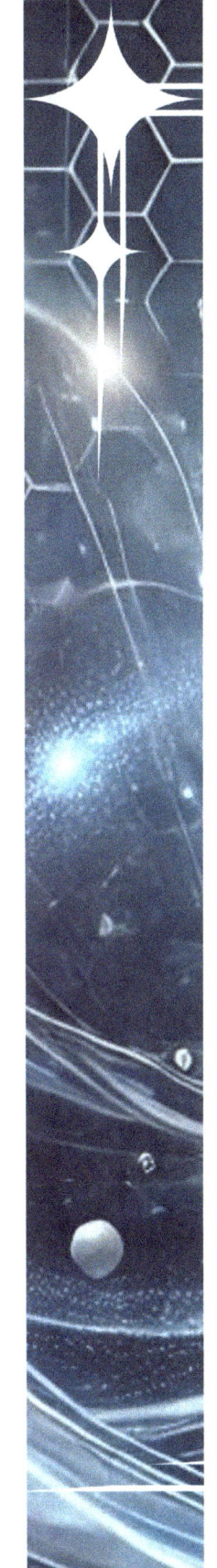

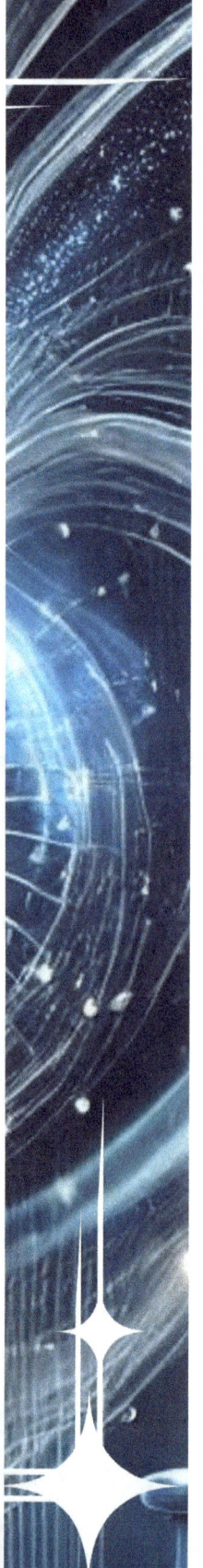

will explore how Tesla's principles are being integrated into contemporary healing modalities, from quantum healing to bioenergetic devices and beyond. We will examine the latest research, technological advancements, and real-world applications that are transforming how we understand and practice medicine.

Beyond Tesla is about more than just honoring Tesla's legacy. It is about pushing the boundaries of what is possible in energy healing. This book serves as both a guide and an invitation to those who are curious about the science behind the unseen forces that govern our health. It is for practitioners looking to integrate these concepts into their practices, researchers eager to explore new frontiers, and anyone intrigued by the potential of energy to transform lives.

Throughout this book, you will discover practical insights, case studies, and emerging trends that illuminate the growing field of energy medicine. As we delve deeper into the principles that Tesla championed, we begin to see that his work was not just about technology but about understanding the very fabric of reality and how it can be harnessed to promote healing and well-being.

As you embark on this journey, keep in mind that the science of energy healing is still unfolding. We stand on the cusp of a new understanding of health—one that honors both the physical and the energetic, the scientific and the spiritual. By advancing the science of energy healing, we are moving closer to realizing Tesla's vision of a future where the power of energy can be fully harnessed for the benefit of all humanity.

Welcome to *Beyond Tesla: Advancing the Science of Energy Healing*.

With continued passion and excitement,

Dr. Constance Santego

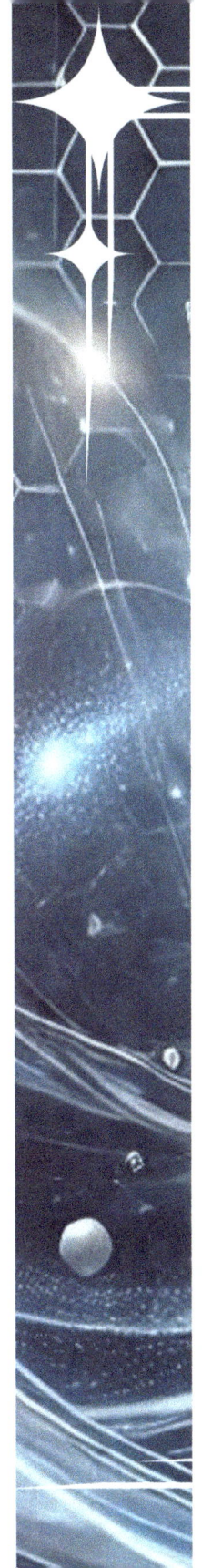

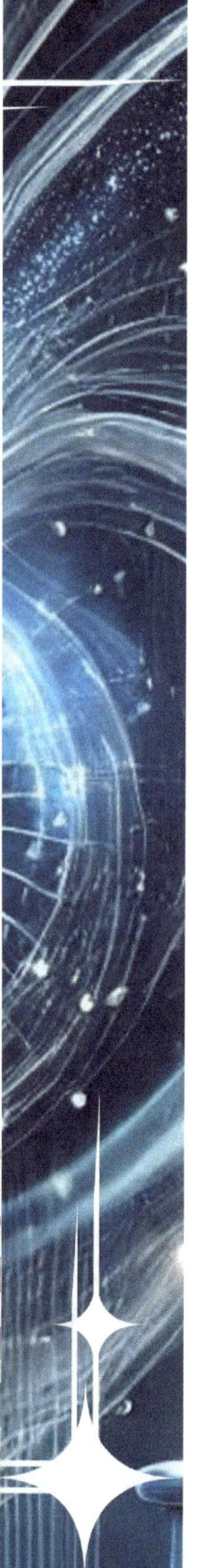

Note to Reader

$\mathcal{D}$ear Reader,

Welcome to *Beyond Tesla: Advancing the Science of Energy Healing*. This book builds upon the foundation established in *Tesla and the Future of Energy Medicine*, delving deeper into the science and philosophy behind Tesla's groundbreaking work and its profound connection to energy healing.

In this second installment, our journey continues beyond the initial exploration of Tesla's visionary ideas, taking you into a deeper understanding of how these principles are actively shaping today's advancements in health, energy medicine, and consciousness. As you embark on this exploration, here are a few notes to enhance your reading experience:

1. **Deepening Your Knowledge**: In *Tesla and the Future of Energy Medicine*, we introduced Tesla's concepts of energy, frequency, and vibration. This book takes that knowledge further, examining how modern science is expanding upon those ideas. As you read, be open to exploring these principles from a scientific and energetic perspective that pushes the boundaries of traditional healthcare.

2. **Bridging Ancient Wisdom and Modern Innovation**: One of the key themes of this book is the convergence of ancient healing traditions and cutting-edge science. You'll find that

energy medicine draws from both, with Tesla's ideas acting as a bridge between them. This book explores how the latest innovations in fields like quantum physics, biofield therapies, and energy-based technologies are connected to both ancient wisdom and modern breakthroughs.

3. **Interdisciplinary Exploration**: *Beyond Tesla* is highly interdisciplinary, integrating insights from quantum mechanics, neuroscience, biology, and holistic medicine. While some of these concepts may be complex, the material is designed to be both thought-provoking and accessible, helping you expand your understanding of energy healing across multiple fields.

4. **Expanding Your Practice**: Though this book is rich with theory, it remains practical in nature. Each chapter offers real-world applications, case studies, and techniques that you can use to enhance your healing practices, whether you are a practitioner or someone interested in your own well-being. The book is meant to inspire you to think critically and creatively about how Tesla's principles can be applied to modern healing methods.

5. **Critical Engagement and Reflection**: The book is not just about absorbing new information—it's about engagement. Reflective questions, advanced thought experiments, and examples of cutting-edge practices are woven throughout the chapters to help you critically assess and apply the material. Use these prompts as opportunities to expand your thinking and challenge your understanding of health, energy, and healing.

6. **Resources for Further Study**: At the end of the book, you'll find resources to continue your

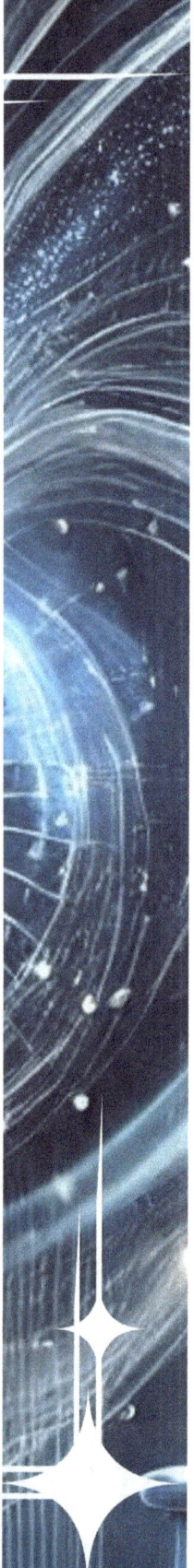

journey. These will help you explore Tesla's influence on energy medicine, dive into the latest scientific developments, and examine how these advancements are influencing the future of healthcare.

7. **Continuing the Conversation**: The field of energy medicine is growing rapidly, and we're just beginning to uncover its full potential. I encourage you to join the conversation, whether through workshops, discussions, or digital platforms, to share your thoughts and experiences as we collectively advance this transformative field.

In *Beyond Tesla*, we move from the theoretical into the applied, from the historical into the present, and begin to glimpse the future of energy medicine. The concepts you'll discover in this book represent the next stage in the evolution of health and healing, where energy is not just a force to be observed but a tool to be harnessed.

Thank you for continuing this journey with me. I hope this book deepens your understanding and inspires you to further explore the limitless possibilities within energy medicine.

With respect and enthusiasm,

Dr. Constance Santego

Learning Outcome

Upon completing *Beyond Tesla: Advancing the Science of Energy Healing*, readers will:

1. **Expand Their Understanding of Tesla's Influence on Cutting-Edge Healing Technologies:**
   - **Explore Tesla's Legacy**: Deepen your knowledge of how Nikola Tesla's theories continue to shape the evolution of energy medicine, from foundational principles to modern advancements in electromagnetic and quantum technologies.

2. **Master Advanced Concepts in Energy Medicine:**
   - **Advanced Knowledge**: Engage with sophisticated ideas, such as quantum healing, advanced biofield therapies, and the latest discoveries on how electromagnetic fields interact with human biology to promote healing.

3. **Integrate Science, Consciousness, and Energy Healing:**
   - **Holistic Understanding**: Learn to synthesize the intersection of scientific research, consciousness studies, and spiritual healing practices into a unified, holistic approach to health and wellness.

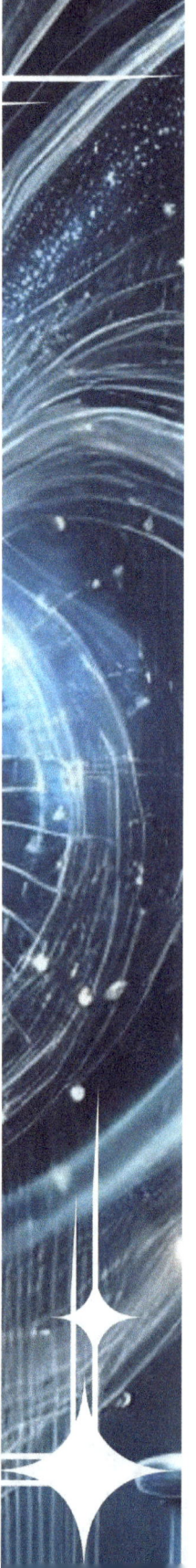

4. **Analyze Groundbreaking Innovations in Energy Medicine:**
   - **Innovation Discovery**: Investigate the newest breakthroughs in energy medicine, including quantum devices, bioenergetic diagnostic tools, and cutting-edge non-invasive therapies that push the boundaries of Tesla's original vision.

5. **Apply Advanced Healing Techniques for Personal and Professional Growth:**
   - **Practical Mastery**: Learn to apply advanced energy medicine methods in both personal wellness and professional settings. This includes techniques for balancing the body's energy systems, using modern energy devices, and facilitating quantum-level healing processes.

6. **Critically Evaluate Ethical, Social, and Environmental Implications:**
   - **Ethical Insight**: Examine the ethical, societal, and environmental considerations tied to emerging energy medicine technologies, while developing strategies to ensure responsible, equitable, and sustainable healing practices.

7. **Shape the Future of Energy Medicine:**
   - **Visionary Thinking**: Cultivate the skills to envision new horizons in energy healing by integrating Tesla's insights with future scientific advancements, helping to guide the evolution of healthcare practices based on energy and frequency.

8. **Foster Lifelong Learning and Expertise in Energy Healing:**
   - **Commitment to Growth**: Be inspired to continue your education in the dynamic field of energy medicine, staying current with ongoing innovations, research, and methodologies that push the limits of healing.

This book equips readers with advanced knowledge, cutting-edge tools, and practical applications to engage fully with the future of energy medicine. By intertwining Tesla's visionary legacy with modern science and technology, readers will be empowered to lead and contribute meaningfully to the ongoing evolution of healthcare and human potential.

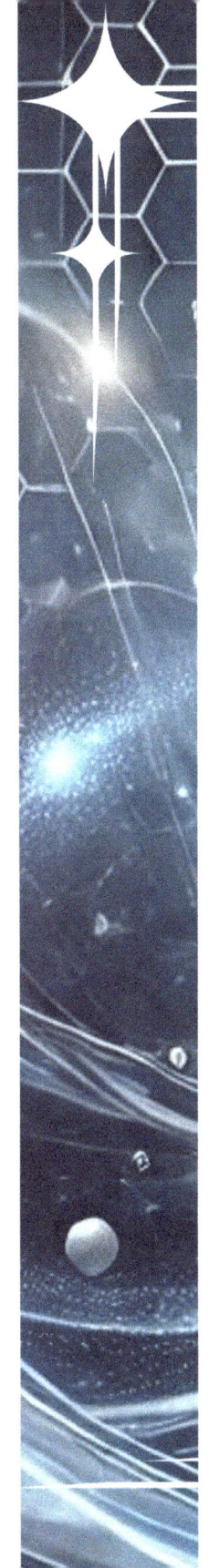

Chapter 1

Tesla's Influence on Modern Healing Technologies

TESLA'S VISION BEYOND ELECTRICITY

Nikola Tesla is celebrated worldwide for revolutionizing electricity with his development of the alternating current (AC) system, a transformative innovation that changed how power was generated and distributed. Yet, Tesla's vision extended far beyond electrifying homes and industries. He foresaw a future where energy—unseen and often misunderstood—would be harnessed not just to power machines but to improve human health and well-being. Tesla believed that by manipulating invisible forces like electromagnetism, humanity could unlock new methods of healing, moving beyond the limitations of traditional medicine.

Tesla's fascination with the unseen forces of nature—energy fields, resonance, and high-frequency currents—laid the foundation for many of the medical technologies that today form the bedrock of modern diagnostics and therapeutic practices. Though Tesla's contributions to this field were not fully appreciated in his time, his work has quietly shaped the trajectory of innovations that we now rely on in healthcare. This chapter explores how Tesla's pioneering discoveries influenced the development of technologies critical to modern medicine and how his vision continues to inspire advancements in healing.

Tesla's Early Work: Laying the Groundwork

Tesla's experiments in electromagnetism were groundbreaking, not only for the world of electrical engineering but also for their potential implications in biological systems. Tesla was one of the earliest visionaries to suggest that electromagnetic fields could directly influence human health—an idea considered radical in his time. Through his experiments with high-frequency currents, most notably demonstrated in his development of the Tesla coil, he showed how powerful electromagnetic fields could penetrate various materials, including human tissue.

Tesla's concept of **resonance**—the idea that all matter vibrates at specific frequencies—hinted at the potential for therapeutic applications. He theorized that by tuning into the body's natural frequencies, one could positively influence health outcomes. Though these ideas were far ahead of his time, they laid the groundwork for what has become a new frontier in medical technology: the use of energy fields for diagnosis and healing.

Tesla's innovations also inspired early electrotherapy experiments, where electrical currents were applied to the body to stimulate healing. These early applications, though rudimentary by today's standards, paved the way for sophisticated modern techniques that leverage the body's inherent electrical properties to promote healing and regeneration. Tesla's drive to explore the intersection of energy and health set the stage for the development of a wide range of medical technologies we now take for granted.

From Theory to Practice: Modern Medical Technologies

Today, Tesla's influence is unmistakable in a host of cutting-edge medical technologies that have revolutionized healthcare. **Magnetic Resonance Imaging (MRI)** is, perhaps, the most notable diagnostic tool that uses strong magnetic fields and radio waves to produce highly detailed images of the body's internal structures. While Tesla did not invent MRI technology, the principles upon which it operates—specifically the use of electromagnetic fields—are directly linked to his work. Tesla's development of the Tesla coil demonstrated the capacity to generate powerful magnetic fields through high-frequency currents, a concept that laid the foundation for modern MRI machines.

Similarly, **laser technology**, now indispensable in modern medicine, owes a debt to Tesla's exploration of electromagnetic waves. Though Tesla did not directly create lasers, his work with directed energy and the transmission of electromagnetic waves provided the theoretical underpinnings for their development. Lasers are now used in an array of medical applications, from eye surgeries and skin treatments to cancer therapy and precision surgeries, echoing Tesla's vision of using energy in focused, controlled ways to achieve specific results.

Tesla's influence also extends to **bioelectromagnetic devices** used in therapeutic settings today. **Transcranial Magnetic Stimulation (TMS),** for example, is a non-invasive treatment that uses magnetic fields to stimulate nerve cells in the brain, particularly in treating depression and other neurological disorders. Similarly, **Pulsed Electromagnetic Field (PEMF) therapy**, which employs electromagnetic fields to promote bone healing and pain relief, can be traced back to Tesla's pioneering work with electromagnetism. These therapies showcase the enduring impact of Tesla's innovations on modern healthcare, illustrating how his early theories have been transformed into life-changing medical practices.

Global Adoption: Tesla's Legacy in Europe

Tesla's impact on medical technology extends beyond the United States, influencing advancements worldwide, particularly in Europe. Countries like Switzerland, Italy, and Germany have become leaders in the development and application of Tesla-inspired technologies, each contributing uniquely to the evolution of energy-based therapies.

- **Switzerland:** Tesla's work is honored in Switzerland through the widespread adoption of high-frequency electromagnetic therapies. Swiss clinics use these therapies for cancer treatment, pain management, and other medical applications, applying principles Tesla first explored. His belief in the healing potential of electromagnetic fields is realized in the Swiss medical landscape, where non-invasive treatment options provide patients with innovative care that aligns with Tesla's vision.
- **Italy:** Italian scientists have advanced bioelectromagnetic research, building on Tesla's pioneering ideas. Italy has contributed to the development of a range of diagnostic and therapeutic devices that use electromagnetic fields to treat neurological disorders and other conditions. Tesla's influence remains a guiding force in Italian medical innovation as researchers continue to explore the healing potential of electromagnetic energy.
- **Germany:** Germany's tradition of integrative and holistic medicine has provided fertile ground for Tesla-inspired technologies. German researchers have developed a variety of bioenergetic devices that align with Tesla's

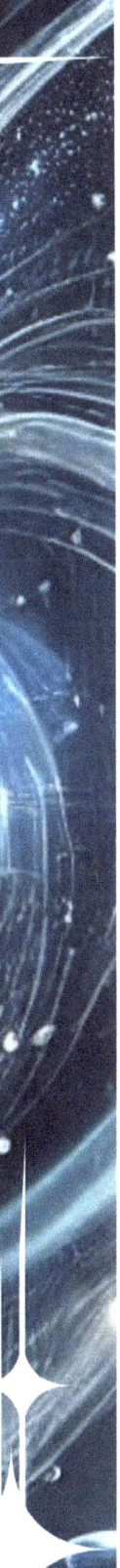

theories on energy and vibration. These devices are used both diagnostically and therapeutically, promoting harmony within the body's energy fields to improve health outcomes. Tesla's vision of health as a holistic interplay of energy resonates deeply with Germany's approach to medicine.

Case Studies: Tesla's Principles in Action

To illustrate Tesla's profound influence on modern healing technologies, the following case studies trace the development of specific medical devices and therapies directly back to Tesla's work:

1. **MRI Machines:** MRI technology, which allows for detailed internal imaging, draws on principles Tesla first demonstrated in his work with magnetic fields and high-frequency currents. The impact of MRI on diagnostics has been revolutionary, allowing doctors to view the body with unprecedented clarity.

2. **Laser Surgery:** Tesla's work with electromagnetic waves laid the theoretical groundwork for lasers, now widely used in eye surgery, cancer treatments, and skin therapies. Tesla's vision of precision energy applications has become a reality in the focused capabilities of modern lasers.

3. **PEMF Therapy:** PEMF therapy, used in treating bone injuries and managing pain, is rooted in Tesla's theories about the beneficial effects of electromagnetic fields on biological tissues. This non-invasive treatment, widely used in hospitals and clinics, showcases the lasting relevance of Tesla's ideas in energy medicine.

Tesla's Enduring Impact on Medicine

Nikola Tesla's contributions to modern medicine may not have been fully realized in his time, but his legacy endures. By laying the conceptual and technological foundations for medical devices and therapies that leverage energy and electromagnetic fields, Tesla has had a lasting impact on healthcare. As medical technologies continue to evolve, Tesla's vision will inspire future innovations, reminding us that the boundaries of science and healing are always expanding, driven by those who dare to imagine the unseen forces that shape our world.

Chapter 2

Expanding the Boundaries of Energy Medicine

Introduction: Tesla's Legacy in Modern Healing Modalities

As the field of energy medicine evolves, new and innovative modalities are emerging that build on foundational principles first explored by pioneers like Nikola Tesla. Tesla's groundbreaking work with energy, frequency, and the electromagnetic spectrum laid the groundwork for many modern healing practices that are reshaping holistic health today. This chapter explores several advanced energy healing modalities, tracing their development back to Tesla's insights and examining their underlying theories and practical applications in healthcare. By diving into these cutting-edge methods, we reveal how deeply rooted Tesla's vision is in modern energy healing and where the field may be headed.

Quantum Healing: Bridging Physics and Consciousness

Quantum healing represents one of the most advanced frontiers in energy medicine, directly reflecting Tesla's understanding of energy and frequency. Rooted in the principles of quantum physics, this modality posits that consciousness itself can influence the physical world, including the body. Quantum healing emphasizes that everything in the universe is composed of energy fields, and that by manipulating these fields, profound healing can be achieved.

Practices such as **meditation, visualization,** and **intention-setting** are central to quantum healing, as they align the body's vibrational state with the quantum field—the very fabric of reality. This section explores the theoretical underpinnings of quantum healing, including Tesla's influence on the understanding of the quantum field, the **observer effect,** and **quantum entanglement**. We also delve into practical applications such as remote healing and energy alignment practices, offering readers a glimpse into how Tesla's ideas are reflected in modern quantum healing.

Biofield Therapies: Harmonizing the Body's Energy Fields

Biofield therapies focus on the body's energy fields, a concept that closely aligns with Tesla's work on electromagnetism and its effects on biological systems. Modalities such as **Healing Touch, Therapeutic Touch,** and **Biofield Tuning** aim to balance the biofield—the energetic field that surrounds and permeates the human body.

Practitioners of biofield therapies use their hands or specialized tools to sense and adjust the energy flow within the biofield, working to clear blockages and restore harmony. This section examines the science behind biofield therapies, exploring how they interact with the body's electromagnetic fields and reviewing the latest research on their efficacy. Practical techniques for incorporating biofield therapies into both personal wellness routines and professional healthcare practices are also discussed, demonstrating their connection to Tesla's early explorations of electromagnetism.

Scalar Energy Healing: Tapping into Subtle Energies

Scalar energy healing is deeply connected to Tesla's exploration of electromagnetic waves. Scalar waves, unlike traditional electromagnetic waves, are nonlinear, multidimensional waves that form standing wave patterns and permeate all of space. These waves are believed to be a limitless source of healing energy, capable of interacting with the body's energy fields to promote deep cellular healing.

This section delves into the origins of scalar energy theory, its direct ties to Tesla's work, and the growing body of research supporting its therapeutic potential. We explore practical applications of scalar energy healing, from the use of scalar devices to their integration into clinical settings, showcasing how Tesla's pioneering ideas are being realized in modern integrative medicine.

Sound Healing: Resonating with Vibrational Medicine

Tesla's fascination with frequency and vibration finds a natural modern counterpart in sound healing, a modality based on the premise that sound waves can restore harmony to the body's energy fields. By resonating with specific frequencies, sound waves help to balance the body and promote healing.

Sound healing techniques involve instruments like **tuning forks, singing bowls,** and **gongs,** which create vibrations that interact with the body's energy systems. These techniques target different aspects of the energy body, from clearing blockages to balancing chakras. This section explores the science behind sound healing, showing how it builds on Tesla's ideas about resonance and energy. We also discuss the latest research on sound healing's efficacy and provide practical guidance for using sound healing tools in both personal and professional settings.

Case Studies: Tesla's Influence in Action

To demonstrate the effectiveness of these advanced energy healing modalities, this section presents case studies from practitioners and patients who have experienced profound results. Each case study highlights how modalities like quantum healing, biofield therapies, scalar energy, and sound healing have been successfully integrated into both traditional and alternative healthcare practices, illustrating the lasting influence of Tesla's vision.

1. **Quantum Healing in Oncology:** This case study examines the use of quantum healing practices to support cancer patients, focusing on improvements in quality of life and emotional well-being, reflecting Tesla's work on energy and consciousness.
2. **Biofield Therapy for Chronic Pain:** This study explores how biofield therapies, grounded in Tesla's electromagnetic principles, have provided relief for patients suffering from chronic pain who did not respond to conventional treatments.
3. **Scalar Energy Devices in Clinical Practice:** A look at how scalar energy devices have been used in integrative medicine clinics to enhance patient outcomes, particularly in treating conditions such as Lyme disease and chronic fatigue syndrome.
4. **Sound Healing for Anxiety and Stress:** A case study on the use of sound healing techniques to alleviate anxiety and stress, demonstrating the physiological and psychological benefits observed in patients, with a focus on Tesla's theories of resonance and vibration.

Tesla's Vision and the Future of Energy Healing

As energy medicine continues to advance, Tesla's influence will undoubtedly shape the next generation of healing modalities. Practitioners and researchers are building upon his pioneering work, offering new paths to health and wellness that align ancient wisdom with cutting-edge science. This chapter has provided a glimpse into the expanding horizons of energy healing, deeply rooted in Tesla's vision, setting the stage for further exploration and innovation in the chapters to come.

Chapter 3

Integrating Energy Medicine into Conventional Healthcare

Introduction: Bridging Two Worlds

As energy medicine gains wider recognition within the medical community, the need to integrate these practices into conventional healthcare systems becomes more pressing. Nikola Tesla's vision of using energy to enhance health laid the foundation for many energy-based therapies that are now becoming more accepted. However, blending these modalities with mainstream medical practices poses both challenges and opportunities. This chapter offers a roadmap for practitioners, patients, and healthcare providers to collaborate and create a more holistic, patient-centered approach to healing.

The Growing Acceptance of Energy Medicine

Once viewed as fringe or alternative, energy medicine is increasingly being integrated into mainstream healthcare. A growing body of research has demonstrated the efficacy of various energy-based modalities, many of which can trace their roots back to Tesla's pioneering work with electromagnetic fields, frequency, and vibration. These therapies are proving effective for conditions like chronic pain, anxiety, cardiovascular disease, and even cancer.

- **Evidence-Based Integration:** Hospitals, clinics, and integrative health centers now offer treatments such as **acupuncture, Reiki,** and

biofeedback as complementary therapies alongside conventional medical interventions. Patient demand, positive clinical outcomes, and the shift toward personalized and holistic care are all driving this trend. This section explores how evidence-based research is validating energy medicine practices, helping to close the gap between conventional and alternative healthcare.

Challenges of Integration: Navigating Different Paradigms

Despite the growing acceptance of energy medicine, integrating these practices into conventional healthcare still presents challenges. The fundamental difference between conventional medicine, which is often rooted in reductionist and evidence-based protocols, and energy medicine, which focuses on holistic and subtle energetic shifts, creates tension in integration efforts.

- **Scientific Validation:** One major challenge is applying conventional scientific standards, such as randomized controlled trials, to energy medicine. Many energy-based practices involve individualized treatments and changes in subtle energy fields, which are difficult to quantify using traditional methods.
- **Professional Acceptance:** Skepticism remains among some medical professionals, often due to a lack of familiarity with or understanding of energy medicine modalities. Bridging this knowledge gap will require ongoing education and open-mindedness.
- **Regulatory and Licensing Issues:** Standardized training, certification, and oversight are essential for ensuring patient safety and efficacy in energy medicine practices. Developing universally accepted credentials will be key in advancing the field.

- **Patient Perception:** Public perception of energy medicine varies, and patients may have different views on its legitimacy and effectiveness. Addressing these concerns with clear communication and education will be important in fostering patient trust.

Successful Models of Integration: Case Studies from Around the World

There are already several successful models for integrating energy medicine into conventional healthcare settings around the world. These examples provide valuable insights into best practices and the benefits of combining holistic and traditional approaches to healing.

- **United States** – Integrative Medicine Centers: Leading institutions like the **Mayo Clinic** and the **Cleveland Clinic** have established integrative medicine centers offering energy-based therapies such as acupuncture, Reiki, and biofeedback. These therapies support patients undergoing treatments for conditions like cancer, chronic pain, and stress-related disorders.
- **Germany** – Complementary Therapies in Oncology: In Germany, cancer treatment centers have successfully integrated energy medicine modalities like **homeopathy, naturopathy,** and **biofield therapies** into oncology care. These therapies complement conventional treatments, helping to reduce side effects and enhance patient well-being.
- **Switzerland** – Integrative Pain Management: Swiss pain management clinics have adopted a multidisciplinary approach that includes energy-based therapies like **Pulsed Electromagnetic Field (PEMF) therapy** and **biofeedback,** particularly for patients with chronic pain who haven't responded to conventional treatments.

- **India** – Ayurvedic and Energy Medicine Integration: In India, the integration of **Ayurveda** with energy medicine practices like **Pranic Healing** and **Reiki** offers a holistic approach to health that combines ancient wisdom with modern energy-based therapies. This model treats the physical, mental, and energetic aspects of well-being.

Practical Guidelines for Integrating Energy Medicine

Successfully integrating energy medicine into conventional healthcare requires a deliberate, collaborative approach. The following guidelines can help healthcare providers and practitioners bridge the gap:

- **Collaborative Care:** Foster open communication and collaboration between conventional healthcare providers and energy medicine practitioners to ensure treatments are complementary and aligned.
- **Education and Training:** Promote education in energy medicine principles for conventional healthcare providers, and vice versa, to create mutual understanding and respect between the two fields.
- **Patient-Centered Care:** Prioritize patient needs, preferences, and values by offering personalized treatment plans that incorporate both conventional and energy-based therapies.
- **Ethical Considerations:** Ensure that energy medicine practices are applied ethically, focusing on patient safety, informed consent, and transparency in treatment outcomes.

The Future of Integrative Healthcare

As the healthcare landscape continues to evolve, the integration of energy medicine into conventional medical systems represents an important step toward more comprehensive, patient-centered care. Bridging the worlds of traditional and energy medicine offers the potential for a healthcare system that not only treats disease but promotes wellness, balance, and harmony at every level of human experience.

Chapter 4

Tesla's Coil: A Visionary Invention and Its Modern Applications

Introduction: The Birth of the Tesla Coil

Nikola Tesla's inventions have long been heralded as groundbreaking, often venturing far beyond the technological capabilities of his time. Among his most iconic creations is the **Tesla coil**, developed in 1891 as an experiment in high-voltage, high-frequency electricity. Tesla envisioned this coil as a way to transmit electricity wirelessly across long distances—an idea that challenged the conventional views of electricity during his era. Although his grand vision of wireless power transmission was not fully realized in his lifetime, the **Tesla coil** has had a lasting impact, influencing various fields including modern medicine, telecommunications, and even space exploration.

In this chapter, we will delve into the history of the **Tesla coil,** examine Tesla's vision for its use, and explore how its principles continue to shape today's cutting-edge technologies. We will also highlight its applications in energy healing and NASA's space exploration efforts.

The Tesla Coil: A Revolutionary Design

The **Tesla coil** is a resonant transformer circuit that generates high-voltage, low-current, high-frequency alternating current electricity. It consists of two key components: a **primary coil** and a **secondary coil,** both of which have their own capacitors. When the primary

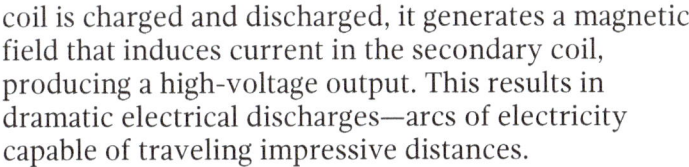

coil is charged and discharged, it generates a magnetic field that induces current in the secondary coil, producing a high-voltage output. This results in dramatic electrical discharges—arcs of electricity capable of traveling impressive distances.

Tesla's coil was revolutionary because it showed the potential for high-frequency electricity to be transmitted without wires. Tesla believed that this technology could one day transmit power wirelessly across the globe, providing energy to remote areas and reducing the need for extensive infrastructure. While his vision of global wireless power transmission was not realized in his time, the Tesla coil became a fundamental tool for further research in electricity and electromagnetism, setting the stage for many modern innovations.

Applications of the Tesla Coil in Medicine

One of the earliest fields to adopt the Tesla coil was medicine. Tesla himself experimented with high-frequency currents, believing they could have beneficial effects on the human body. His work paved the way for what later became known as **diathermy**, a treatment using high-frequency electromagnetic currents to generate heat within body tissues, promoting healing and providing pain relief.

Today, modern adaptations of Tesla's design are used in medical devices that stimulate tissues through electromagnetic fields. **Pulsed Electromagnetic Field (PEMF) therapy**, for example, shares many similarities with Tesla's early experiments. PEMF therapy is now widely used for bone healing, pain management, and treating musculoskeletal conditions, proving that Tesla's ideas still have a significant impact on contemporary medicine and energy healing.

The Tesla Coil's Influence on Telecommunications and Power Transmission

Although Tesla's dream of global wireless power transmission has yet to be realized, the underlying principles of the **Tesla coil** have had a profound impact on telecommunications. The ability of the coil to generate high-frequency signals contributed to the development of early radio technology, enabling the transmission of signals over long distances. Tesla's work directly influenced radio pioneers such as **Guglielmo Marconi,** who is often credited with developing the first practical radio communication systems.

In the realm of power transmission, Tesla's ideas continue to inspire modern research. Scientists today are exploring ways to transmit power wirelessly, drawing on the principles Tesla pioneered. These include innovations like wireless charging systems for consumer electronics and electric vehicles, as well as space-based solar power systems designed to beam energy back to Earth. Tesla's work in this area continues to resonate, demonstrating his lasting influence on both telecommunications and energy transmission.

The Tesla Coil and Space Exploration: Applications by NASA

Tesla's influence reaches beyond Earth to the realm of space exploration. **NASA** has explored several technologies that draw on Tesla's ideas, particularly in the development of wireless power systems and **high-frequency electrical systems for spacecraft.**

One of the most promising applications of Tesla's work in space is **electromagnetic propulsion.** Researchers are experimenting with high-frequency electromagnetic fields—similar to those generated by **Tesla coils**—to propel spacecraft without conventional fuel. This technology, often referred to as **electric propulsion**, has the potential to revolutionize space travel by reducing the need for heavy fuel loads, making long-duration missions more sustainable.

Additionally, Tesla's contributions to high-frequency electromagnetic fields have informed the development of **space communication systems.** These systems must operate under extreme conditions, transmitting signals across vast distances without interference. The resilience and efficiency of high-frequency transmissions, as explored by Tesla, remain crucial for successful space missions.

Case Studies: Modern Uses of Tesla's Coil Design

To further illustrate the enduring impact of Tesla's work, this section presents case studies of contemporary technologies that have been inspired by or directly utilize the principles of the **Tesla coil.**

- **Diathermy in Modern Medicine:** Tesla's early work with high-frequency currents evolved into diathermy, a medical treatment still widely used today. Diathermy promotes healing by using electromagnetic energy to generate heat within body tissues.
- **Wireless Charging Technologies:** Tesla's vision of wireless power transmission has had a profound influence on the development of wireless charging systems, now commonly used for smartphones, electric vehicles, and other consumer electronics.
- **Electromagnetic Propulsion for Spacecraft:** NASA continues to explore electromagnetic propulsion systems based on Tesla's ideas, aiming to use high-frequency electromagnetic fields to propel spacecraft, potentially revolutionizing space travel.
- **High-Frequency Communication Systems:** Tesla's work with high-frequency electromagnetic fields informs the design of advanced communication systems used in both terrestrial and extraterrestrial applications.

The Legacy of the Tesla Coil

The **Tesla coil** remains one of Nikola Tesla's most iconic inventions, symbolizing his genius and far-reaching vision. While the coil did not achieve the widespread application Tesla originally imagined, its influence is undeniable. From medicine to telecommunications, power transmission to space exploration, the principles embodied in the **Tesla coil** continue to shape the technologies of today and tomorrow.

Tesla's work stands as a testament to the power of innovation, a reminder that ideas can transcend their time and push the boundaries of what is possible. The legacy of the **Tesla coil** and its enduring influence highlights the transformative potential of energy in our world, offering glimpses of what the future may hold.

Chapter 5

The Intersection of Consciousness and Energy Healing

Introduction: The Role of Consciousness in Healing

For centuries, consciousness has intrigued philosophers, scientists, and spiritual practitioners alike. Its role in health and healing, particularly within the realm of energy medicine, has become an area of growing interest. The deeper we explore the mysteries of human health, the more we realize that consciousness plays a pivotal role in the healing process. This chapter delves into how consciousness interacts with energy fields and how this interaction can be harnessed to promote healing and well-being. We will explore various theories of consciousness, their implications for energy medicine, and practical insights on how these concepts can be applied in both personal and professional healing practices.

Understanding Consciousness: Theories and Perspectives

Consciousness is typically described as the awareness of one's existence, thoughts, and surroundings. However, its true nature remains one of the most profound and elusive aspects of human experience. Multiple theories have emerged to explain consciousness, each offering unique perspectives:

- **Materialist Theories:** These theories posit that consciousness arises from the brain's complex neural interactions. In this view, consciousness is an emergent property of brain activity and ceases when brain activity stops.

- **Dualist and Non-Dualist Theories:** Dualism suggests that consciousness and the physical body are separate entities, with consciousness existing independently of the brain. Non-dualism, by contrast, sees consciousness as an indivisible aspect of reality, interwoven with all phenomena.
- **Quantum Consciousness:** A more recent theory links consciousness to quantum processes. Proponents argue that the brain operates at a quantum level, with consciousness emerging from the interplay between quantum mechanics and biological processes.

This section unpacks these theories, examining their relevance to energy medicine. Understanding consciousness from these diverse viewpoints provides profound insights that can significantly enhance healing practices.

The Mind-Body Connection: Consciousness as a Healing Tool

The mind-body connection is a cornerstone of many healing traditions and plays a critical role in energy medicine. A growing body of scientific evidence supports the idea that the mind can influence the body and vice versa. Practices such as meditation, visualization, and mindfulness have been shown to affect physical health, influencing everything from stress levels to immune function.

In energy medicine, the mind is often viewed as a tool that can direct and manipulate energy within the body. For example, **visualization techniques** guide the flow of energy through the body's meridians or chakras, directing it toward areas in need of healing. Similarly, **intention-setting** allows the patient or practitioner to consciously focus on a specific healing outcome, amplifying the effects of energy-based treatments.

This section will explore how consciousness can be used as a healing tool, offering practical examples and techniques that readers can apply. Scientific evidence from fields like **psychoneuroimmunology** and **neuroplasticity** will provide a deeper understanding of how the mind influences the body's energy systems.

Quantum Healing: Consciousness and the Quantum Field

Quantum healing bridges the gap between quantum physics and consciousness studies. It suggests that consciousness can influence the **quantum field**—the fundamental realm where particles and energy interact in ways that defy classical physics. Quantum healing theory draws from the **observer effect,** a quantum phenomenon in which observation alters the state of a particle. This principle suggests that by consciously focusing on desired outcomes, one can influence the quantum field and, by extension, promote healing.

Practices such as **meditation** and **visualization** allow practitioners to enter deep states of awareness and intentionally direct consciousness toward healing. By aligning one's consciousness with the quantum field, proponents believe it is possible to affect the energy patterns that shape physical health, leading to profound healing outcomes.

In this section, we'll explore the principles of quantum healing and its application in energy medicine. We will also touch on the ongoing scientific debates surrounding quantum healing, presenting both supportive evidence and criticisms to offer a balanced view of this innovative field.

The Power of Belief: Placebo, Nocebo, and Consciousness

The **placebo effect**—in which a patient's belief in a treatment's effectiveness leads to real improvements—underscores the profound role that consciousness plays in healing. Conversely, the **nocebo effect** occurs when negative expectations cause a worsening of symptoms. Both phenomena highlight the powerful influence of belief and expectation on physical health.

Understanding these effects is crucial in energy medicine. Practitioners must recognize how belief can either enhance or undermine the effectiveness of treatments. This section explores the mechanisms of the placebo and nocebo effects and how they can be harnessed in energy healing. We'll also discuss the ethical implications of working with patients who may be influenced by these effects, particularly regarding transparency and informed consent.

Case Studies: Consciousness in Action

This section presents real-world case studies that demonstrate the practical application of consciousness in energy healing:

1. **Healing Through Visualization:** A case study detailing how a patient used visualization techniques to aid in the recovery from a serious illness, showing the impact of conscious intent in directing the body's energy.
2. **Mindfulness and Chronic Pain:** An exploration of how mindfulness practices have helped manage chronic pain, focusing on the relationship between consciousness, perception, and physical sensation.
3. **Quantum Healing in Practice:** A look at quantum healing principles in a clinical setting, examining patient outcomes and their experiences with energy healing.
4. **The Power of Belief in Treatment Outcomes:** A case study that reveals how positive and

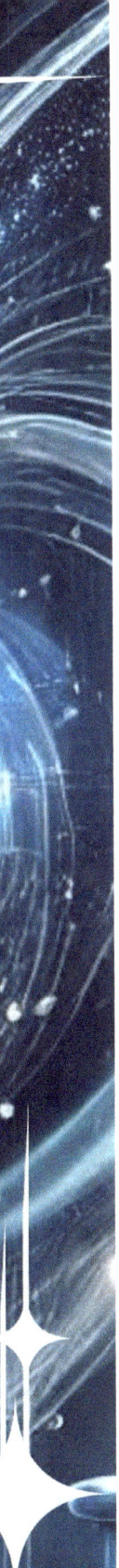

negative expectations affected the results of an energy medicine intervention, highlighting the significant role of consciousness in healing.

The Future of Consciousness in Healing

As our understanding of consciousness continues to evolve, its role in health and healing is becoming more prominent in both conventional and alternative medicine. The potential of consciousness to influence physical health opens new avenues for research and clinical practice, offering a more holistic approach to healing that integrates mind, body, and spirit.

The future of energy medicine will likely see greater recognition of consciousness as a healing force, paving the way for more comprehensive and integrative treatments that honor the power of both the human mind and the energetic field.

Chapter 6

Ethical Considerations in Energy Medicine

Introduction: The Importance of Ethics in Healing

As energy medicine gains broader recognition and acceptance, addressing the ethical considerations surrounding its practice becomes essential. Ethics form the foundation of responsible healing practices, ensuring the protection of patients' rights, safety, and well-being. This chapter will explore the key ethical challenges faced by energy medicine practitioners and offer guidelines on maintaining professional integrity. By fostering a deep understanding of ethical principles, practitioners can build trust with their patients and contribute to the credibility and advancement of energy medicine within the healthcare field.

Informed Consent: Empowering Patients with Knowledge

Informed consent is fundamental to ethical healthcare practice. It ensures that patients are fully aware of the treatments they will receive, including the potential benefits, risks, and available alternatives. In the realm of energy medicine, informed consent is particularly crucial because of the subtle nature of many therapies and the general public's unfamiliarity with them.

Practitioners must explain energy medicine modalities in simple, accessible terms. This explanation should cover how the treatment works, what patients can expect during the session, and any potential side effects or limitations. Practitioners should encourage an open dialogue, allowing patients to ask questions and express concerns.

This section will provide practical steps for obtaining informed consent in energy medicine. Special attention will be given to the challenges practitioners may face, such as cultural differences and varied perceptions of energy healing, and how to navigate these with sensitivity and respect.

Confidentiality and Privacy: Protecting Patient Information

Confidentiality is a cornerstone of ethical healthcare, ensuring that a patient's personal information remains private. In energy medicine, confidentiality extends beyond conventional medical records to include personal, spiritual, or emotional details shared during treatment.

Practitioners must adhere to strict confidentiality protocols, ensuring all information is securely stored and shared only with the patient's explicit consent. This section will explore the ethical and legal responsibilities surrounding confidentiality in energy medicine, offering practical advice on maintaining privacy and building a trusting therapeutic relationship.

Boundaries and Professionalism: Navigating Dual Relationships

Maintaining appropriate boundaries is critical in all therapeutic relationships, but it is especially important in energy medicine, where practitioners and patients may share a deep emotional or spiritual connection. Practitioners need to be mindful of potential dual relationships, where personal connections outside the therapeutic context could influence the healing process.

This section will discuss the importance of setting and maintaining boundaries to protect the patient and ensure the integrity of the treatment. It will also address common scenarios where boundary issues may arise, such as in small communities or among friends and family members, and offer strategies for navigating these situations professionally.

Competence and Continuing Education: Staying Informed and Skilled

To practice ethically, energy medicine practitioners must remain competent and up-to-date in their field. Energy medicine is rapidly evolving, and ongoing education ensures that practitioners are equipped with the latest knowledge and techniques to provide high-quality care.

This section will emphasize the importance of professional development and lifelong learning in energy medicine. It will cover ways practitioners can stay informed through workshops, professional organizations, peer supervision, and research. The ethical implications of practicing beyond one's scope of competence and the importance of making appropriate referrals when necessary will also be addressed.

Cultural Sensitivity: Respecting Diversity in Healing Practices

Energy medicine is practiced within diverse cultural contexts, each with its own healing traditions and beliefs. Practitioners must approach every patient with cultural sensitivity, recognizing and respecting diverse perspectives on health, illness, and healing.

This section will provide guidance on practicing cultural sensitivity in energy medicine. Tips for effective communication and strategies for building rapport with patients from various cultural backgrounds will be offered. Additionally, it will highlight the ethical responsibility practitioners have to educate themselves about the cultural contexts they operate in and to seek consultation or training when necessary.

Addressing Misuse and Misrepresentation: Upholding Integrity in the Field

As energy medicine grows in popularity, the potential for misuse or misrepresentation increases. Some individuals may offer energy medicine services without proper training or ethical grounding, which can harm patients and undermine the credibility of the field.

This section will discuss the ethical challenges related to the misuse of energy medicine, such as making false claims, exploiting vulnerable populations, or commercializing healing practices inappropriately. Practitioners have an ethical responsibility to uphold the field's integrity by adhering to high standards and addressing unethical behavior when encountered. The role of self-regulation and peer accountability in maintaining public trust will also be explored.

Case Studies: Ethical Dilemmas in Energy Medicine

To illustrate the ethical challenges practitioners face, this section presents case studies that highlight common ethical dilemmas in energy medicine:

1. **Informed Consent in a Culturally Diverse Setting:** A case study exploring the challenges of obtaining informed consent from a patient with a different cultural background and how the practitioner handled this situation with care and sensitivity.
2. **Boundary Issues in a Small Community:** A case study examining the ethical complexities of treating a patient with whom the practitioner had a dual relationship and the steps taken to maintain professionalism and boundaries.

3. **Addressing Misrepresentation in the Field:** A case study discussing how a practitioner dealt with a colleague making exaggerated claims about their qualifications and treatment outcomes, exploring the ethical implications of addressing this behavior.

Conclusion: Building a Trustworthy and Ethical Practice

Ethics are the bedrock of a trustworthy and effective energy medicine practice. By upholding ethical principles, practitioners can foster respectful relationships with their patients, enhance the credibility of the field, and ensure positive healing outcomes. This chapter has outlined the key ethical considerations in energy medicine, providing guidance for navigating these challenges with integrity.

As energy medicine continues to evolve, practitioners must remain vigilant in upholding ethical standards. Doing so will ensure that energy medicine is respected as a vital part of the healthcare landscape, offering safe and effective treatments to all who seek healing.

Chapter 7

Introduction: Energy Medicine Around the World

Energy medicine, with roots in ancient healing traditions and modern scientific discoveries, has evolved into a global movement. As the understanding of the body's energetic systems grows, cultures worldwide are integrating energy medicine into their healthcare systems in unique and innovative ways. This chapter explores the worldwide impact of energy medicine, highlighting how various cultures embrace these practices and how cross-cultural exchanges continue to shape the future of healing. By examining the diverse approaches to energy medicine globally, we can gain a deeper appreciation for its universal principles and how it adapts to meet the specific needs of different populations.

Traditional Healing Practices and Energy Medicine

Many cultures possess long-standing healing traditions focused on the manipulation of energy within the body. These time-honored practices form the foundation of modern energy medicine and continue to influence contemporary approaches to health and wellness.

- **Traditional Chinese Medicine (TCM):** In China, the concept of "Qi" (or "Chi")—the vital life force flowing through the body's meridians—has been central to TCM for thousands of years. Practices like acupuncture, qigong, and herbal medicine are based on regulating and balancing Qi. This section explores how TCM's principles have shaped modern energy medicine, particularly in developing modalities such as acupuncture and acupressure, now widely practiced globally.

- **Ayurveda in India:** Ayurveda, the ancient Indian system of medicine, is centered on achieving balance among the body's energies, known as "doshas." Ayurveda incorporates diet, lifestyle, herbal remedies, and energy-based techniques like Pranic Healing to maintain this balance. This section examines how Ayurveda's holistic approach to health and energy has shaped the integration of mind, body, and spirit in modern energy medicine practices.

- **Indigenous Healing Traditions:** Indigenous cultures worldwide have their own energy-based healing traditions rooted in a deep connection to nature and the spiritual world. For instance, Native American practices use ceremonies, drumming, and sacred plants to harness healing energy, while African traditional healers utilize spiritual and energetic techniques to restore balance within individuals and communities. This section highlights how these indigenous practices contribute to the broader field of energy medicine and offer a unique blend of physical and spiritual healing.

The Integration of Energy Medicine in Western Healthcare

In Western countries, energy medicine is increasingly being integrated into mainstream healthcare as part of complementary and alternative medicine (CAM). This section explores how energy medicine is gaining acceptance in Western healthcare systems, the challenges it faces, and the benefits it offers patients.

- **The United States:** Energy medicine is becoming more common in U.S. hospitals,

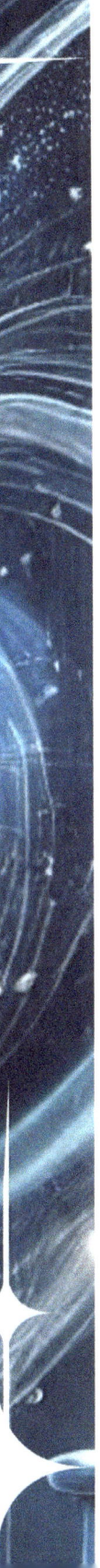

clinics, and wellness centers. Integrative medicine programs now include therapies like Reiki, Healing Touch, and biofeedback as part of a holistic approach to patient care. This section discusses the growing demand for energy medicine in the U.S., supported by patient satisfaction, positive clinical outcomes, and increasing scientific validation.

- **Europe:** European countries, such as the United Kingdom, Germany, and France, have embraced energy medicine, particularly within integrative and complementary therapies. In Germany, for example, energy medicine is used alongside conventional treatments in oncology and pain management. This section examines how different European healthcare systems integrate energy medicine, with a focus on public perception, regulation, and the role of evidence-based practices.

- **Australia and New Zealand:** In Australia and New Zealand, energy medicine is part of a larger movement toward holistic health. Energy-based therapies like kinesiology, Bowen therapy, and sound healing are gaining popularity. This section explores how these countries' emphasis on natural health supports the incorporation of energy medicine into mainstream healthcare.

Cross-Cultural Exchanges and the Evolution of Energy Medicine

The global spread of energy medicine has fostered significant cross-cultural exchanges, where healing practices from different traditions merge to create new, innovative modalities. This section explores how these exchanges contribute to the evolution of energy medicine and the emergence of groundbreaking healing practices.

- **Fusion of East and West:** The blending of Eastern and Western healing methods is one of the most significant trends in the development of energy medicine. For example, acupuncture, once a strictly Eastern practice, has been incorporated into Western medicine and is often combined with techniques like biofeedback and physical therapy. This section explores how such fusions create comprehensive, effective healing modalities.

- **Global Conferences and Collaborations:** International conferences, workshops, and online platforms have become important venues for sharing energy medicine techniques and knowledge. Practitioners from around the world gather to exchange ideas, learn from one another, and collaborate on new healing practices. This section highlights key global events and collaborations shaping the future of energy medicine.

- **Innovation Through Cultural Synergy**: As energy medicine spreads across borders, new modalities are emerging that draw on multiple cultural traditions. For instance, sound healing practices may combine Tibetan singing bowls with Western music therapy, while energy healing techniques might integrate Ayurvedic principles with modern bioenergetics. This section explores how cultural synergy is driving innovation in energy medicine, leading to a fusion of ancient wisdom with cutting-edge science.

Case Studies: Global Success Stories in Energy Medicine

To illustrate the global impact of energy medicine, this section presents case studies from various countries that showcase successful integrations and innovative practices emerging from cross-cultural exchanges.

1. **Integrative Oncology in Germany:** A case study highlighting how a German oncology clinic has integrated energy medicine into its

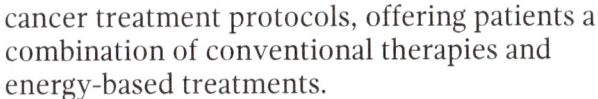

cancer treatment protocols, offering patients a combination of conventional therapies and energy-based treatments.

2. **Ayurvedic Energy Healing in India:** An exploration of how Ayurvedic principles are being used in energy medicine practices in India, focusing on integrating Pranic Healing with Ayurveda in both urban and rural healthcare settings.

3. **Acupuncture and Biofeedback in the U.S.: A** look at how a U.S. integrative medicine center combines acupuncture with biofeedback and mindfulness techniques to treat chronic pain and manage stress.

4. **Indigenous Healing Practices in Australia:** A case study of how Aboriginal healing practices are being incorporated into energy medicine therapies in Australia, blending traditional knowledge with modern healing techniques.

The Universal Language of Energy

Energy medicine has become a global phenomenon, with practices that transcend cultural boundaries while adhering to universal principles of healing. As energy medicine continues to evolve, it is shaped by the diverse cultural traditions from which it draws and the innovations that arise through cross-cultural exchanges. This chapter has provided a glimpse into how different cultures approach healing and how these approaches are converging to form a more holistic and integrated healthcare field.

Looking ahead, the continued exchange of knowledge and practices will be essential for the advancement of energy medicine. By embracing its diversity and learning from one another, we can create a more inclusive, compassionate, and effective approach to healing—one that honors the wisdom of the past while harnessing the possibilities of the future.

Chapter 8

The Future of Energy Medicine: Trends, Innovations, and Possibilities

Introduction: Charting the Course for the Future

Energy medicine is at a transformative crossroads where ancient wisdom intersects with cutting-edge scientific advancements. As we look toward the future, emerging trends, innovations, and potential breakthroughs promise to reshape the landscape of healthcare, pushing the boundaries of how we understand and facilitate healing. This chapter delves into these developments, offering a visionary perspective on how energy medicine may redefine health and healing in the years ahead.

Emerging Technologies in Energy Medicine

Technological advancements are rapidly propelling energy medicine into new realms of possibility, enabling more precise and effective treatments than ever before. This section explores some of the most promising emerging technologies that will likely shape the future of energy medicine.

- **Bioenergetic Devices:** As our understanding of the human energy field deepens, innovative bioenergetic devices are being developed to detect and treat energetic imbalances with increasing accuracy. These devices utilize sensors and advanced algorithms to measure subtle energy patterns and offer targeted interventions. Wearable technologies, for example, monitor and optimize the body's energy field in real-time, potentially revolutionizing how we manage health.

- **Quantum Healing Technologies:** Quantum healing is an area of growing interest, rooted in the convergence of quantum physics and energy medicine. Advances in quantum computing and nanotechnology are creating new opportunities for quantum healing devices, which operate at the most fundamental levels of energy. These technologies may pave the way for personalized energy medicine treatments tailored to an individual's unique energetic profile, offering profound potential for healing.
- **Non-Invasive Diagnostic Tools:** The future of energy medicine is likely to see the development of sophisticated non-invasive diagnostic tools capable of assessing health through the body's energy fields. These tools, which include advanced imaging technologies, could visualize energy systems and detect imbalances before they manifest as physical symptoms, offering a proactive approach to preventive medicine.

Integrative Approaches: Bridging Energy Medicine with Conventional Healthcare

The future of healthcare lies in integrating energy medicine with conventional medical practices, creating a more comprehensive and holistic approach to healing. This section examines the evolving potential for blending these modalities to provide enhanced care.

- **Collaborative Care Models:** The rise of collaborative care models is likely, where energy medicine practitioners and conventional healthcare providers work together to create personalized, holistic treatment plans. These models would merge the strengths of both fields, offering patients a broader range of treatment options to address complex health needs.

- **Energy Medicine in Mainstream Healthcare:** As energy medicine gains more scientific validation, it is increasingly likely to be integrated into mainstream healthcare settings. Energy-based therapies could become standard treatments for managing chronic pain, mental health disorders, and other conditions, reflecting a shift toward a more personalized and patient-centered approach to medicine.
- **Training and Education:** The successful integration of energy medicine into conventional healthcare will require the development of standardized training programs and certification processes. This ensures that healthcare professionals are adequately trained in energy medicine modalities, leading to safe, effective, and scientifically grounded treatments.

Personalized Energy Medicine: The Rise of Individualized Care

Personalized medicine represents one of the most exciting possibilities for the future of energy medicine, allowing treatments to be tailored to the specific needs of individual patients. Advances in both technology and our understanding of human energy fields are making this shift toward individualized care increasingly feasible.

- **Genomic and Energetic Profiling:** As genomic science converges with energy medicine, new profiling tools may emerge that enable practitioners to design treatments based on a patient's genetic and energetic makeup. This could lead to highly targeted interventions that minimize side effects while maximizing therapeutic outcomes, transforming the way we approach healing.

- **Customizable Treatments:** The future of energy medicine will likely involve customizable treatment modalities, such as bioenergetic devices and quantum healing technologies, designed specifically for each patient's energetic profile. These tailored approaches offer the potential for more effective and individualized care, shifting the healthcare paradigm toward precision energy medicine.
- **Holistic Health Management:** Personalized energy medicine may become part of a broader trend toward holistic health management, where patients actively participate in monitoring and adjusting their energetic health. With tools like wearable devices, mobile apps, and other technologies, patients will be empowered to stay in tune with their energy needs, fostering self-awareness and long-term well-being.

Ethical Considerations for the Future

As energy medicine continues to evolve and adopt new technologies, it is critical to address the ethical implications of these advancements. This section explores some of the key ethical challenges that will arise as energy medicine continues to develop.

- **Privacy and Data Security:** With the rise of bioenergetic devices and personalized energy treatments, safeguarding patient privacy and securing sensitive health data will become paramount. As more healthcare services rely on digital platforms, practitioners will need to ensure that data is protected from breaches and misuse.
- **Accessibility and Equity:** As energy medicine technologies become more advanced, there is a risk that these treatments could be accessible only to those who can afford them, exacerbating health inequalities. Practitioners

and healthcare systems must take steps to ensure that energy medicine remains inclusive, with equitable access to cutting-edge treatments for all patients.

- **Informed Consent and Autonomy:** The complexity of future energy medicine treatments may make it difficult for patients to fully understand their options and make informed decisions. Ensuring patient autonomy will require clear communication and an emphasis on informed consent, empowering patients to take an active role in their own healing process.

Case Studies: Innovations Shaping the Future of Energy Medicine

To illustrate the possibilities discussed in this chapter, the following case studies present examples of innovative technologies and practices that are currently shaping the future of energy medicine.

1. **Wearable Bioenergetic Devices:** This case study explores a wearable device designed to monitor the body's energy field and provide real-time feedback, helping patients maintain optimal energy levels and overall health.
2. **Quantum Healing Clinics:** A look into a pioneering clinic that uses quantum healing technologies to treat various conditions, offering insights into how quantum healing may transform future healthcare practices.
3. **Personalized Energy Medicine Programs:** This case study highlights a program that combines genomic and energetic profiling to create individualized treatment plans for patients with chronic illnesses, demonstrating the potential of personalized energy medicine.
4. Integrative Healthcare Models: An examination of a healthcare system that has successfully integrated energy medicine into its standard care practices, showcasing the potential for

collaborative care models to enhance patient outcomes.

The Visionary Future of Energy Medicine

The future of energy medicine is filled with exciting possibilities that hold the potential to revolutionize healthcare. By embracing emerging technologies, integrating energy medicine with conventional practices, and focusing on personalized, patient-centered care, energy medicine can offer more effective, holistic, and compassionate treatments.

As we continue to push the boundaries of what is possible in energy medicine, it is vital to remain committed to ethical practice and patient well-being. By doing so, we can ensure that energy medicine evolves in a way that benefits humanity, offering new pathways to health, healing, and transformation.

Chapter 9

Cutting-Edge Magnetic Technologies in Energy Medicine

Introduction: The Power of Magnetics in Healing

Magnetic therapy has long been valued for its potential to promote healing, alleviate pain, and enhance overall well-being. Recent advancements in technology have placed magnetic therapy at the forefront of modern energy medicine. Companies like Mas Magnetics, PureWave, and Seqex are leading the charge with innovative products designed to harness magnetic fields for therapeutic purposes. This chapter explores how these cutting-edge technologies are shaping the future of energy medicine and offering new pathways to holistic health.

1. Mas Magnetics: Innovating Magnetic Therapy

Mas Magnetics stands at the forefront of magnetic therapy, offering a range of products engineered to deliver therapeutic benefits through high-quality static magnets. Their wearable devices and magnetic pads target specific areas of the body, providing focused magnetic fields that help alleviate pain, reduce inflammation, and promote wellness.

Mas Magnetics' products interact with the body's natural magnetic and energetic systems, enhancing cellular function and circulation. Frequently used alongside energy medicine practices such as acupuncture, Reiki, and biofield therapies, Mas

Magnetics' solutions are integral to many practitioners' holistic healing protocols.

2. PureWave: Pioneering Pulsed Electromagnetic Field Therapy

PureWave specializes in Pulsed Electromagnetic Field (PEMF) therapy, which uses electromagnetic fields to stimulate cellular repair and regeneration. PEMF is a non-invasive, scientifically-backed therapy shown to be effective in managing chronic pain, accelerating bone healing, and treating neurological disorders.

PureWave's product range includes portable PEMF devices for personal use and advanced systems for clinical applications. Known for their versatility and ease of use, these devices make PEMF therapy accessible to a wide range of users. Supported by numerous studies, PEMF therapy improves circulation, reduces inflammation, and promotes tissue regeneration, making it a valuable modality in energy medicine.

3. Seqex Mats: Advanced Magnetotherapy from Italy

Seqex represents the cutting edge of electromedical technology with their advanced magnetotherapy mats developed in Italy. These mats apply controlled pulsed or variable electromagnetic fields to the body, stimulating biological processes that support healing. The core technology behind Seqex mats is ion resonance, allowing for personalized treatments suitable for both clinical and home use.

Seqex mats are distinguished by their compliance with international safety standards, making them highly versatile for a variety of therapeutic applications. For practitioners seeking comprehensive care options, Seqex mats integrate seamlessly into holistic treatment plans, enhancing patient outcomes.

Comparative Analysis: Mas Magnetics, PureWave, and Seqex

While Mas Magnetics, PureWave, and Seqex all harness magnetic fields for therapeutic benefits, their approaches and technologies vary:

Technology and Application:

- Mas Magnetics focuses on static magnetic fields, which are ideal for targeted pain relief and general wellness.
- PureWave specializes in dynamic PEMF therapy, which is best suited for deep tissue regeneration.
- Seqex offers a more customizable approach, combining ion resonance technology for treating both acute and chronic conditions.

User Experience and Accessibility:

- All three companies prioritize ease of use and accessibility, making their products suitable for home and professional settings.
- Seqex stands out for its customizable options, appealing to practitioners who require flexible treatment methods.

Effectiveness and Research Support:

- PureWave's PEMF therapy and Seqex's ion resonance technology are well-supported by scientific research.
- Mas Magnetics is gaining recognition for its effectiveness in pain relief, which is supported by positive patient outcomes.

Case Studies: Real-World Applications of Magnetic Therapy

To highlight the practical impact of these technologies, the following case studies illustrate how Mas Magnetics, PureWave, and Seqex products are being successfully used in energy medicine practices.

Chronic Pain Management with Mas Magnetics: A patient suffering from chronic pain experienced significant relief using Mas Magnetics' wearable devices. The targeted magnetic fields reduced inflammation and improved mobility, demonstrating the product's effectiveness in managing long-term pain.

PEMF Therapy for Bone Healing with PureWave: PureWave's PEMF devices were used in a clinical setting to accelerate bone healing for a patient recovering from a fracture. The non-invasive therapy promoted faster regeneration and reduced discomfort, showcasing PEMF's value in orthopedic recovery.

Integrative Treatment Plans with Seqex: An energy medicine practitioner incorporated Seqex mats into their holistic practice, combining magnetotherapy with other modalities such as acupuncture and biofield therapy. The customizable treatment plans enhanced patient outcomes, especially for those with chronic conditions.

The Future of Magnetic Therapy in Energy Medicine

As magnetic therapy continues to evolve, its role in energy medicine will likely expand. Future trends include advancements in magnetic field technology, broader research and clinical trials, and increased accessibility for a wider range of patients. Companies like Mas Magnetics, PureWave, and Seqex are at the forefront of these developments, ensuring that magnetic therapy remains a vital tool in holistic healthcare.

The Role of Magnetic Technologies in Holistic Healing

Magnetic therapy, exemplified by the innovative products from Mas Magnetics, PureWave, and Seqex, represents a powerful and non-invasive approach to healing. By harnessing the natural properties of magnetic fields, these technologies complement other energy-based modalities in the quest for holistic health. As research continues to validate the benefits of magnetic therapy and new advancements emerge, magnetic technologies are poised to become an integral part of holistic healthcare, offering patients and practitioners new avenues for achieving well-being and vitality.

Chapter 10

The Synergy of Science and Spirituality in Energy Medicine

Introduction: Bridging Two Worlds

Energy medicine sits at the intersection of science and spirituality, blending empirical research with ancient wisdom to create a holistic healing approach that addresses the mind, body, and spirit. In this chapter, we explore how scientific advancements and spiritual practices work in harmony within energy medicine, offering a comprehensive understanding of health and well-being that transcends traditional medical models.

The Role of Science in Validating Energy Medicine

As energy medicine grows in popularity, scientific research is increasingly focused on validating its efficacy. Studies on biofield therapies, magnetotherapy, and other energy-based modalities are providing evidence that these treatments can positively impact health outcomes. This section highlights key findings from recent research and how these discoveries support integrating energy medicine into mainstream healthcare.

- **Research on Biofield Therapies**: Studies have shown that therapies like Reiki, Healing Touch, and Therapeutic Touch can reduce stress, alleviate pain, and improve overall well-being. This section reviews findings that support the effectiveness of biofield therapies in clinical settings, demonstrating their ability to complement conventional treatments.

- **Advancements in Magnetotherapy:** Scientific research into magnetotherapy is rapidly advancing, with studies confirming how magnetic fields influence cellular processes and promote healing. This section explores the mechanisms by which magnetotherapy works and its growing role in modern energy medicine as a tool for pain relief and tissue regeneration.

Spirituality and Energy Medicine: A Holistic Approach

While science provides the framework to understand how energy medicine works, spirituality offers a philosophical and ethical foundation. Spirituality in energy medicine reflects the interconnectedness of life and acknowledges that health is not simply the absence of illness but a state of harmony within oneself and with the universe.

- **The Spiritual Dimension of Healing**: Spiritual practices—such as meditation, prayer, and intention-setting—enhance the healing process by fostering inner peace and connection. These practices align the body's energy with universal principles, amplifying the effects of energy medicine. This section explores how spirituality complements energy medicine, enriching the healing experience.
- **Integrating Spirituality into Practice:** For practitioners, incorporating spiritual elements into their energy medicine practices can deepen the healing experience. This section offers practical guidance on how to respect diverse spiritual beliefs while using meditation, mindful intention, and compassionate care to enhance patient outcomes.

Case Studies: The Synergy in Action

To demonstrate the powerful combination of science and spirituality in energy medicine, this section presents case studies where integrating these two dimensions has led to profound healing outcomes.

1. **Healing Chronic Illness Through Integrated Approaches:** This case study highlights a patient managing a chronic condition through a combination of magnetotherapy, biofield therapy, and spiritual practices such as meditation and visualization. The combined approach significantly improved the patient's quality of life, demonstrating the synergy between these modalities.
2. **Transformative Healing in Palliative Care:** Energy medicine, supported by spiritual care, has provided comfort and enhanced the quality of life for patients in palliative care settings. This case study showcases how integrating energy-based therapies with spiritual support can offer transformative relief for those nearing the end of life.
3. **Stress Reduction and Emotional Healing:** This case study explores how combining biofeedback with spiritual practices such as mindfulness has helped patients manage stress and achieve emotional balance. The blend of scientific tools and spiritual practices highlights the complementary nature of both approaches in addressing emotional and physical health.

The Future of Energy Medicine: A Unified Approach

The future of energy medicine lies in the continued integration of scientific research and spiritual wisdom. As our understanding of the body's energy systems grows, it becomes increasingly important to honor the spiritual traditions that have guided healing practices for millennia.

- **Educational Initiatives:** To create a unified approach to energy medicine, training programs must educate practitioners on both the scientific and spiritual aspects of energy healing. This section discusses the need for holistic education that enables healthcare professionals to offer a more integrated, patient-centered approach to care.
- **Collaborative Research:** Collaboration between scientists and spiritual practitioners offers a new frontier in energy medicine. By combining empirical data with spiritual insight, we can explore areas such as consciousness, the nature of healing, and the mind-body connection. This section highlights the potential for joint research efforts that honor both scientific and spiritual perspectives, fostering a deeper understanding of energy medicine.

Embracing the Whole

Energy medicine presents a unique opportunity to bridge the gap between science and spirituality, offering a holistic path to healing that honors both empirical research and experiential wisdom. By embracing this integrated approach, practitioners can offer more comprehensive and compassionate care, helping patients achieve true well-being.

As we look to the future, the continued fusion of science and spirituality will be essential to unlocking the full potential of energy medicine. This synergy ensures that energy medicine remains a respected and effective component of modern healthcare, capable of addressing the complex needs of individuals seeking balance, healing, and harmony.

Chapter 11

The Next Frontier in Energy Medicine

Introduction: Pioneering New Pathways

Energy medicine is on the brink of remarkable advancements, moving beyond its current practices into uncharted territories. This chapter explores the next frontier in energy medicine, focusing on innovative trends, emerging technologies, and visionary perspectives that promise to redefine our approach to healing. By delving into the latest breakthroughs, we aim to inspire practitioners, researchers, and healthcare professionals to push the boundaries of what's possible in this evolving field.

Emerging Trends in Energy Medicine

Several key trends are shaping the future of energy medicine, reflecting both the expansion of existing practices and the rise of new approaches.

- **AI and Machine Learning in Energy Medicine:** Artificial intelligence (AI) and machine learning are revolutionizing many areas of healthcare, and energy medicine is no exception. These technologies enable the analysis of vast data sets, identifying patterns that enhance diagnostic precision and treatment effectiveness. This section examines how AI is being integrated into energy medicine, from predictive diagnostics to personalized treatment planning, making energy therapies more efficient and accessible.

- **Nanotechnology and Energy Medicine:**
Nanotechnology is set to play a pivotal role in energy medicine by enabling interventions at the cellular and molecular levels. Nanoparticles can interact with the body's energy systems to deliver targeted therapies. This section explores how nanotechnology can revolutionize energy medicine, offering highly precise and minimally invasive treatments.
- **The Rise of Telehealth in Energy Medicine:**
The global shift toward digital healthcare is increasingly evident in energy medicine, where telehealth is becoming an essential tool. Virtual consultations, remote diagnostics, and energy-based digital therapies are making energy medicine more accessible. This section discusses how telehealth is transforming energy medicine, enabling practitioners to reach a global audience and offer personalized care from a distance.

Innovative Technologies on the Horizon

As technological innovation accelerates, new tools and devices are emerging that promise to reshape energy medicine. These breakthroughs represent quantum leaps in the field, enhancing both the precision and scope of energy-based healing.

- **Quantum Field Generators:** Rooted in the principles of quantum physics, quantum field generators emit frequencies that resonate with the body's natural energy systems, aiming to correct energetic imbalances. This section explores the science behind these devices and their potential applications in treating both chronic and acute conditions.
- **Holographic Healing Technologies:**
Holographic healing leverages light and sound waves to create holograms that interact with the body's energy fields. These holograms can be programmed to target specific health issues,

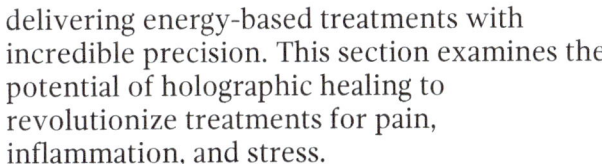

delivering energy-based treatments with incredible precision. This section examines the potential of holographic healing to revolutionize treatments for pain, inflammation, and stress.

- **Wearable Energy Devices:** Wearable devices that monitor and influence the body's energy fields are opening new possibilities for self-care and preventive medicine. These devices provide real-time feedback on energy levels, stress, and overall well-being, allowing individuals to take a more active role in managing their health. This section discusses the most promising wearable energy devices and their potential to reshape personal healthcare.

Visionary Perspectives: The Future of Healing

Visionary thinkers in energy medicine are constantly pushing the envelope, exploring the profound connections between consciousness, energy, and healing. This section presents some of the most forward-thinking ideas that will likely shape the future of energy medicine.

- **Integrating Consciousness and Energy Medicine:** There is a growing interest in how shifts in consciousness can influence the body's energy fields. Researchers are exploring the relationship between conscious thought, intention, and physical healing, aiming to understand how the mind can be harnessed to enhance energy-based treatments. This section delves into the latest theories and experimental work in this area.
- **Global Collaboration for Advancing Energy Medicine:** The future of energy medicine will be shaped by international collaboration. Practitioners, researchers, and educators from across the globe are working together to share knowledge and develop unified approaches to

energy healing. This section explores how global partnerships are driving innovation and expanding the reach of energy medicine.

- **The Role of Education in Shaping the Future:** As energy medicine evolves, so does the need for education that bridges traditional healing with cutting-edge science. This section discusses the importance of creating educational programs that equip future practitioners with the skills and knowledge to lead in this rapidly changing field.

Case Studies: Exploring New Frontiers

To showcase the potential of the next frontier in energy medicine, this section presents case studies that highlight pioneering work in the field.

1. **AI-Driven Energy Medicine Treatments:** A case study of a clinic using AI to design personalized energy medicine treatments, demonstrating how AI enhances precision and treatment outcomes.
2. **Nanotechnology in Cellular Healing:** An exploration of a research project using nanotechnology to deliver energy-based treatments at the cellular level, showcasing the potential for minimally invasive therapies that target illness at its source.
3. **Holographic Healing for Chronic Conditions:** A look at a pilot program using holographic healing to treat chronic pain and inflammation, illustrating the potential of this emerging technology in managing difficult-to-treat conditions.

Embracing the Infinite Possibilities

The next frontier of energy medicine is vast, and the possibilities are boundless. With the integration of cutting-edge technologies, visionary ideas, and global collaboration, the future holds transformative potential for healthcare. This chapter has explored the

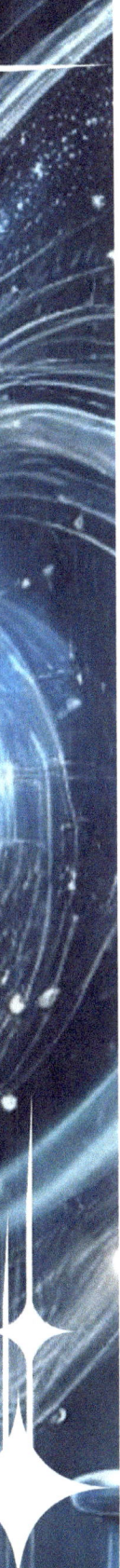

trends, innovations, and perspectives that will shape the future of energy medicine, offering a glimpse into a world where healing is more precise, personalized, and effective than ever before.

As energy medicine continues to evolve, the challenge will be to embrace these new possibilities while maintaining the core principles of holistic, patient-centered care. By doing so, practitioners and researchers can lead the way in transforming healthcare, not only for the benefit of individuals but for the betterment of society as a whole.

Chapter 12

Integrating Energy Medicine into Daily Life

Introduction: Making Energy Medicine Accessible

Energy medicine, with its profound potential to enhance health and well-being, is not confined to clinics or specialized practitioners. The principles and practices of energy medicine can be seamlessly integrated into daily life, empowering individuals to take charge of their health in a holistic and meaningful way. This chapter focuses on practical applications of energy medicine that anyone can incorporate into their routines, promoting balance, vitality, and resilience.

Daily Practices for Energy Balance

Incorporating energy medicine into daily life can be as simple as adopting consistent practices that help maintain harmony within the body's energy systems. These practices are designed to be accessible to everyone, regardless of prior experience with energy healing.

- **Morning Energy Activation:** Starting the day with energy activation practices can set a positive tone and prepare the body for the day ahead. Simple exercises like energy tapping, meridian stretching, or deep breathing techniques can awaken the body's energy pathways.

- **Grounding Techniques**: Grounding, or connecting with the earth's energy, is essential for maintaining stability and balance. Techniques such as walking barefoot on natural surfaces, practicing mindful breathing outdoors, or using grounding mats at home can align the body's energy with the earth, reducing stress and enhancing well-being.
- **Energy Cleansing Rituals:** Throughout the day, the body can accumulate energetic stress that may lead to feelings of tension or fatigue. Simple cleansing rituals like taking salt baths, practicing mindful visualization, or engaging in gentle movement can help refresh and revitalize your energy.

Enhancing Well-Being with Energy Medicine Tools

Various tools and devices have been developed to support energy medicine practices, making it easier for individuals to engage with their energy health regularly.

- **Mindfulness and Meditation Apps:** With the rise of digital health tools, several apps offer guided meditations, breathing exercises, and mindfulness practices to help users manage stress and cultivate inner peace.
- **Sound Healing Instruments:** Instruments like tuning forks or singing bowls are used in sound healing to balance the body's energy through specific frequencies. Learning to use these tools at home can be a powerful way to promote relaxation and harmony.
- **Biofeedback Devices:** Biofeedback technology allows individuals to monitor physiological functions such as heart rate variability, helping them become more aware of their body's responses and facilitating stress management.

Integrating Energy Medicine into Self-Care Routines

Self-care is crucial for maintaining health and well-being, and integrating energy medicine into these routines can enhance their effectiveness.

- **Mindful Movement:** Practices like yoga, tai chi, and qigong integrate physical movement with breath and mindfulness, promoting the flow of energy through the body and supporting both physical and energetic health.
- **Meditation and Visualization:** Meditation helps focus the mind and direct energy where it is needed most. Visualization techniques, such as imagining healing light or grounding roots, can amplify the benefits of meditation, making it a powerful tool for daily energy management.
- **Nutrition and Energy:** The foods we eat influence our energy levels and overall vitality. Incorporating a balanced diet rich in whole foods like fruits, vegetables, and whole grains supports the body's energy systems. Staying hydrated and mindful eating practices also contribute to optimal energy balance.

Creating an Energetically Harmonious Living Space

The environment in which we live plays a significant role in our energy health. Creating a space that supports positive energy flow can enhance well-being and promote harmony.

- **Optimizing Your Space:** Arranging your living environment to promote comfort and reduce clutter can positively affect your energy levels. Incorporating elements of nature, such as plants or natural light, can enhance the ambiance.
- **Clearing and Refreshing Your Space:** Regularly refreshing your living space can prevent the buildup of stress and promote a

peaceful atmosphere. Practices like opening windows for fresh air, using calming scents, or playing soothing music can contribute to an energetically supportive environment.

- **Creating Personal Reflection Areas:** Setting up a dedicated space for relaxation or meditation can serve as a focal point for your energy practices. Personalizing this area with meaningful items can enhance its significance in your daily routine.

Incorporating Energy Medicine into Family Life

Energy medicine can be a valuable tool for entire families. Teaching children about mindfulness and involving family members in energy practices can promote a sense of unity and well-being.

- **Family Mindfulness Practices:** Engaging in group activities like family meditation, deep-breathing exercises, or gentle yoga can strengthen family bonds and create a supportive environment for everyone's well-being.
- **Teaching Children About Mindfulness:** Introducing children to concepts like deep breathing, gratitude, and mindful awareness can empower them to manage stress and emotions effectively.

Case Studies: Personal Journeys in Energy Medicine

1. **Managing Stress Through Daily Practices:** This case study follows an individual who incorporated morning energy activation and grounding techniques into their routine, leading to significant reductions in stress and anxiety.
2. **Enhancing Family Well-Being:** A look at a family that adopted group mindfulness practices and created a harmonious living

space, resulting in improved communication and emotional well-being.

3. **Personal Growth Through Energy Practices:** An exploration of how one person's journey with meditation and mindful movement facilitated personal growth and increased resilience.

Empowering Yourself with Energy Medicine

Integrating energy medicine into daily life is a powerful way to take control of your health and well-being. By incorporating simple practices and routines, you can maintain balance, enhance vitality, and cultivate a deeper connection to yourself and the world around you. This chapter has provided a roadmap for making energy medicine an accessible and integral part of everyday life, empowering you to live with greater awareness and harmony.

Remember that these practices are about consistent effort and intention rather than perfection. By making energy medicine a regular part of your life, you can unlock its full potential and experience the profound benefits it offers.

Step-by-Step Guide: Morning Energy Activation Practice

(38 Exercises will be taught in the next book, *Tesla's Code: Mastering Energy, Frequency, and Creative Power*).

Objective: To start your day with energy activation techniques that awaken your body's energy pathways, set a positive tone, and prepare you for the day ahead.

Duration: 5-10 minutes

Step 1: Centering Breath

- Find a Comfortable Position: Sit or stand comfortably with your spine straight and feet grounded.
- Deep Breathing: Inhale deeply through your nose, filling your lungs completely. Hold your breath for a moment, then exhale slowly through your mouth.
- Repeat 3-5 Times: Focus on your breath, allowing each inhalation to bring in fresh energy and each exhalation to release tension.

Step 2: Gentle Stretching

- Neck and Shoulder Rolls: Gently roll your neck and shoulders to release tension.
- Arm Stretches: Extend your arms overhead and stretch upward, feeling the elongation in your spine.
- Side Stretches: Lean gently to each side, stretching the muscles along your torso.

Step 3: Energy Tapping

- Thymus Tap: Using your fingertips, gently tap the center of your chest (about two inches below your collarbone) for 20-30 seconds

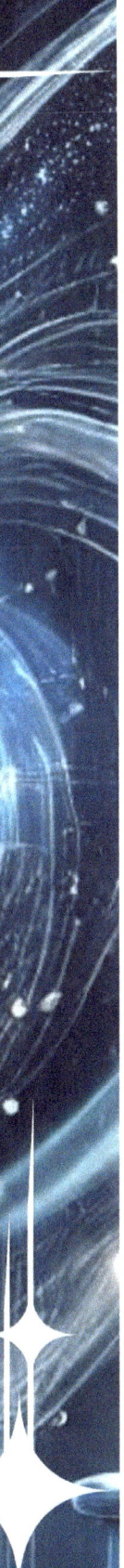

while breathing deeply. This area is associated with immune system support.

- Acupressure Points: Gently massage or tap acupressure points, such as the area between your eyebrows or just below your eyes, to stimulate energy flow.

Step 4: Grounding Visualization

- Visualize Roots: Imagine roots growing from the soles of your feet deep into the earth.
- Connect with Earth Energy: As you inhale, visualize drawing up nourishing energy from the earth into your body. As you exhale, release any tension or negativity down through your roots.
- Maintain for 1-2 Minutes: Continue this visualization, feeling grounded and energized.

Step 5: Setting Intentions

- Choose a Positive Affirmation: Select an affirmation that resonates with you, such as "I embrace the day with energy and enthusiasm" or "I am centered and grounded."
- Repeat Silently or Aloud: Repeat your affirmation several times, focusing on its meaning and allowing it to uplift your mindset.
- Set a Daily Intention: Reflect on what you hope to achieve or experience during the day, setting a clear and positive intention.

By incorporating this Morning Energy Activation routine into your daily life, you can enhance your overall energy levels, improve focus, and cultivate a positive mindset to carry throughout your day. Feel free to adapt this practice to suit your personal needs, and enjoy the benefits of starting your day with mindful energy.

Chapter 13

Creating a Community of Healing and Innovation

Introduction: The Power of Collective Healing

As energy medicine continues to grow and evolve, the importance of building strong, supportive communities becomes increasingly evident. Healing is not only an individual journey but also a shared experience that can be greatly enhanced through collaboration and collective intention. This chapter explores the role of community in energy medicine, highlighting how creating networks of healing, learning, and innovation can foster a more holistic approach to health and well-being. Whether you're a practitioner, patient, or enthusiast, building connections within the energy medicine community can provide invaluable support and inspiration on your healing journey.

The Importance of Connection in Healing

Energy medicine emphasizes the interconnectedness of all life, and this principle extends to the relationships we form within our communities. Healing is often more effective and long-lasting when it occurs in a supportive environment, where individuals can share their experiences, exchange knowledge, and uplift one another.

- **The Healing Power of Group Energy:** Group energy healing sessions, such as group meditation or collective energy work, can amplify the effects of individual healing practices. The combined intention and focus of a group create a powerful, energetic field that supports each participant's healing journey. This section explores the benefits of group energy healing and provides guidelines for organizing group sessions.

- **Building a Network of Support:** Whether through local meetups, online communities, or social media groups, finding like-minded individuals who share your interest in energy medicine can create a sense of belonging and mutual support. This section discusses the value of joining or creating energy medicine communities, offering advice on where to find these networks and how to engage meaningfully within them.

- **Collaborative Healing Practices:** Collaborative approaches to healing, such as practitioner co-treatments or interdisciplinary healing teams, can provide a more comprehensive and tailored experience for patients. This section explores how practitioners from different backgrounds can work together to integrate energy medicine into a broader healthcare approach.

Fostering Innovation Through Community Collaboration

The collective wisdom of the energy medicine community is one of its greatest strengths. By coming together, practitioners and researchers can share insights, explore new ideas, and develop innovative approaches to healing. Fostering a culture of collaboration within the community is essential for the continued growth and advancement of energy medicine.

- **Global Conferences and Retreats:** International conferences, workshops, and retreats offer practitioners the opportunity to learn from experts, share their own knowledge, and collaborate on new research. This section highlights key global events in the energy medicine field and discusses the importance of attending such gatherings to stay connected with emerging trends and innovations.

- **Research Collaborations and Case Study Sharing:** Collaborative research efforts allow energy medicine practitioners and scientists to pool their knowledge and resources, creating more robust and comprehensive studies. This section encourages practitioners to participate in or initiate collaborative research projects and emphasizes the value of sharing case studies to further validate the effectiveness of energy medicine modalities.

- **Educational Networks and Peer Support:** Creating educational networks that offer mentorship, continuing education, and peer support can help practitioners stay updated on the latest advancements in energy medicine. This section discusses the role of professional organizations, online courses, and peer support groups in fostering ongoing learning and development.

The Role of Technology in Building Energy Medicine Communities

Advancements in technology have made it easier than ever to build and maintain energy medicine communities. Online platforms, social media, and telehealth services are transforming the way individuals connect, share knowledge, and receive healing.

- **Online Healing Communities:** With the rise of social media and online platforms, individuals can now join energy-healing communities from anywhere in the world. These communities provide a space for members to share experiences, ask questions, and learn from one another. This section offers tips on how to find reputable online healing communities and how to contribute meaningfully to these groups.

- **Telehealth and Virtual Healing Sessions:** Telehealth services are making energy medicine more accessible to people who may not have access to local practitioners. Virtual healing sessions allow practitioners to offer their services to clients worldwide, expanding the reach of energy medicine. This section explores the rise of telehealth in energy medicine, providing guidelines for practitioners on how to offer virtual sessions effectively.

- **Crowdsourcing Ideas and Innovation:** Crowdsourcing platforms enable practitioners, researchers, and innovators to gather feedback, ideas, and resources from a larger community. This section discusses how energy medicine practitioners can leverage crowdsourcing to develop new tools, techniques, and modalities that address the evolving needs of the community.

Creating a Sacred Space for Community Healing

The environment in which healing occurs plays a critical role in the process. Whether it's an online space or a physical location, creating a sacred, intentional space for healing can enhance the community's ability to support one another on their healing journeys.

- **Creating a Healing Sanctuary:** Whether you're hosting group sessions in your home, studio, or online, the physical and energetic space you create can deeply influence the experience. This section provides guidelines for setting up an energetically supportive environment that fosters connection, healing, and peace.

- **Rituals and Intentions for Group Healing:** Rituals, such as opening and closing ceremonies, can enhance the focus and intention of group healing work. This section offers ideas for simple but powerful rituals that can be incorporated into group healing sessions to strengthen the collective energy and ensure a safe and sacred space for all participants.

Case Studies: Communities of Healing and Innovation

This section presents case studies from various energy medicine communities that have successfully fostered healing and innovation through collaboration, shared wisdom, and collective intention.

- **The Healing Collective:** A case study of a community-led energy medicine center that offers collaborative treatments, group healing sessions, and educational workshops, showcasing the power of collective healing.
- **Global Telehealth Network:** An exploration of an international network of energy medicine practitioners who use telehealth to reach clients worldwide, illustrating how technology can build global communities of healing.
- **Innovation through Collaboration:** A look at a research project where energy medicine practitioners and scientists collaborate to explore new modalities, resulting in groundbreaking discoveries and techniques.

Building a Future of Healing Together

The future of energy medicine will be shaped not only by individual practitioners but by the strength of the communities they build. By fostering a spirit of collaboration, innovation, and mutual support, we can create a more inclusive and effective approach to healing that honors the wisdom of the past while embracing the possibilities of the future.

As you continue your journey in energy medicine, remember that healing is not an isolated endeavor. By engaging with others, sharing your knowledge, and learning from the collective wisdom of the community, you can deepen your practice and contribute to the continued growth of energy medicine as a powerful force for good in the world.

Through community, we find strength, inspiration, and a shared commitment to healing ourselves and the planet.

Chapter 14

The Role of Energy Medicine in Personal and Collective Transformation

Introduction: Energy Medicine as a Catalyst for Change

Energy medicine holds the potential not only to heal the body and mind but also to transform individuals and communities at a deeper, more profound level. This chapter explores the role of energy medicine in personal and collective transformation, focusing on how energy practices can lead to spiritual growth, emotional resilience, and a greater sense of connectedness. We will also examine how these personal transformations contribute to larger shifts in society, promoting healing and harmony on a global scale.

Personal Transformation through Energy Medicine

Energy medicine goes beyond the treatment of physical ailments. It offers a pathway to personal transformation by fostering a deeper understanding of the self, enhancing emotional well-being, and awakening spiritual awareness.

- **Healing Beyond the Physical:** Energy medicine provides a holistic approach to health, addressing the emotional, mental, and spiritual aspects of well-being. This section discusses how energy healing modalities, such as Reiki, acupuncture, and chakra balancing, can help individuals process trauma, release emotional blockages, and cultivate inner peace. By focusing on the energetic roots of physical symptoms, energy medicine empowers individuals to heal from within, leading to profound personal change.

- **Spiritual Awakening and Energy Alignment:** Many energy medicine practices encourage individuals to connect with their higher selves and the universal energy that surrounds us. Practices such as meditation, breathwork, and sound healing help raise one's vibrational frequency, fostering a greater sense of purpose, clarity, and spiritual awakening. This section explores how energy medicine facilitates spiritual growth, offering individuals the tools to align with their true selves and live more consciously.

- **Building Emotional Resilience:** Energy medicine teaches individuals how to manage their energy systems, creating emotional resilience and mental clarity. Techniques such as grounding, energy protection, and mindfulness empower individuals to navigate life's challenges with greater ease and balance. This section delves into the specific energy practices that enhance emotional resilience and provide long-term mental health benefits.

Collective Healing and Transformation

While energy medicine has the power to transform individuals, its influence can extend beyond the personal realm, affecting families, communities, and even global systems. Collective healing through energy work can foster deeper connections between people, creating environments where compassion, understanding, and harmony thrive.

- **Group Energy Practices for Collective Healing:** Group energy work can amplify healing outcomes, creating a shared energetic

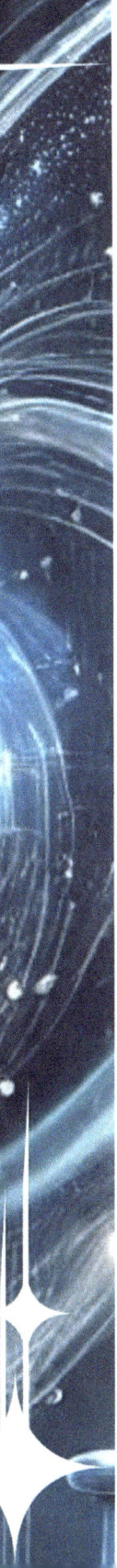

space where collective intentions for peace, health, and well-being can manifest. Whether through group meditation, synchronized energy healing sessions, or community rituals, collective energy practices can raise the vibrational frequency of entire communities. This section explores how group energy practices are being used to support community healing and foster a sense of unity.

- **The Ripple Effect of Personal Transformation:** Personal transformation often leads to changes in the collective consciousness. As individuals heal and evolve, they contribute to the larger shifts occurring in society. This section highlights how the healing of one person can positively impact those around them, creating a ripple effect that leads to broader cultural, social, and environmental transformation.

- **Energy Medicine and Social Change:** As energy medicine practitioners and healers work to elevate individual consciousness, there is also a growing movement to apply these principles to social change. Energy medicine can be used to address systemic issues such as inequality, environmental degradation, and global conflict by shifting the collective energy toward healing and balance. This section discusses how energy practitioners are using their skills to contribute to movements for social justice, peace, and sustainability.

Energy Medicine for Global Healing

In today's interconnected world, the health of individuals and communities is directly tied to the health of the planet. Energy medicine offers a unique perspective on how we can address global challenges by healing the energy of the Earth and fostering global unity.

1. **Healing the Earth's Energy:** Just as individuals have energy fields, so too does the Earth.

Practices such as earth healing, geomancy, and environmental energy clearing focus on restoring balance to the planet's energy systems. This section explores how energy medicine practitioners are working to heal the Earth's energy grid, promoting environmental sustainability and ecological harmony.

2. **Creating a Global Community of Healers:** The power of energy medicine lies in its ability to connect people across cultures, religions, and borders. As practitioners and patients engage with energy healing modalities, they become part of a global network of healers who are committed to raising the vibrational frequency of the planet. This section discusses how global energy healing communities are collaborating to support planetary healing, from synchronized global meditations to international healing initiatives.

3. **The Vision for Global Unity:** Energy medicine's ultimate goal is to foster unity—between individuals, within communities, and across the globe. This section explores how the principles of energy medicine can be applied to global peace-building efforts, offering a vision of a world where healing, compassion, and love are the guiding forces.

Case Studies: Collective and Global Transformations through Energy Medicine

This section presents case studies that highlight the transformative power of energy medicine on both personal and collective levels.

1. **Community Healing Circles:** A case study of a community that regularly hosts energy healing circles to support collective healing, improve local well-being, and foster deeper connections between members.

2. **Global Meditation for Peace:** An exploration of a global synchronized meditation event that

aimed to raise the vibrational frequency of the planet, resulting in reports of increased peace and harmony in participants' lives.

3. **Healing the Earth's Energy Grid:** A case study of a group of energy practitioners who worked together to heal the energy grid of a region suffering from environmental degradation, showcasing how energy medicine can contribute to environmental restoration.

Embracing Energy Medicine for a Better World

Energy medicine is not just a tool for personal healing; it is a pathway to collective transformation and global unity. By integrating energy medicine into daily life, fostering community healing, and working toward planetary well-being, we can create a world that is more harmonious, compassionate, and aligned with the principles of love and balance.

As we move forward into the future, energy medicine offers a vision of a world where healing is not limited to the individual but where the health of the collective—humanity and the planet—takes center stage. By embracing this holistic vision of healing, we can co-create a future where the physical, emotional, spiritual, and planetary realms are all in balance, working together for the good of all.

This final chapter reminds us that while energy medicine begins with the self, its true potential lies in its ability to transform the world around us. Let us harness the power of energy medicine to heal ourselves, our communities, and our planet as we step into a new era of global harmony and collective well-being.

Appendices

Glossary of Terms

Acupuncture: An ancient Chinese medicine technique involving the insertion of needles into specific points on the body to balance the flow of Qi (vital energy) through pathways known as meridians.

Alternating Current (AC): A type of electrical current in which the direction of the flow of electrons switches back and forth at regular intervals or cycles. Tesla's development of the AC electricity supply system was one of his most significant contributions to modern electrical engineering.

Aura: An energy field believed to surround living beings, often perceived as layers of color, representing various aspects of an individual's physical, emotional, and spiritual health.

Bioelectromagnetic (BEM) Therapy: A form of alternative medicine that involves the use of electromagnetic fields to treat and heal various conditions, based on the premise that electromagnetic interventions can influence cellular and physiological processes.

Biofield: A term used in holistic medicine to describe a field of energy and information that surrounds and permeates the human body, playing a role in health and healing.

Chakras: According to ancient Indian medicine, these are energy centers within the body that help to regulate all its processes, from organ function to the immune system and emotions.

Craniosacral Therapy: A gentle, hands-on approach that releases tensions deep in the body to relieve pain and dysfunction, improving whole-body health and performance by manipulating the synarthrodial joints of the cranium.

Electromagnetic Field (EMF): Physical fields produced by electrically charged objects affect the behavior of charged objects in the vicinity of the field.

Energetic Hygiene: Practices aimed at cleansing, protecting, and balancing one's personal energy field or biofield. Examples include grounding, energy shielding, and regular meditation.

Energy Medicine: A branch of alternative medicine based on the belief that healers can channel healing energy into a patient and effect positive results.

Frequency: In the context of energy healing, it refers to the specific rate at which energy or vibrations oscillate or repeat.

Grounding (Earthing): The practice of connecting physically to the Earth's surface electrons by walking barefoot outside, which is believed to promote physiological and electrophysiological changes beneficial for health.

Hertz (Hz): The unit of frequency in the International System of Units (SI), which measures the number of cycles per second of any periodic phenomenon.

Kirlian Photography: A technique used to capture the phenomenon of electrical coronal discharges, often marketed as a way of visualizing a person's aura or biofield.

Meridians: In traditional Chinese medicine, these are invisible pathways in the body along which vital energy flows. Blockages or imbalances in this flow are thought to cause illness and disease.

Qi (Chi): In Chinese philosophy, it's the life force or vital energy that flows through all living things. It is the central underlying principle in Chinese traditional medicine and martial arts.

Quantum Healing: A holistic healing approach that draws on principles of quantum mechanics, suggesting that health can be restored through shifts in consciousness and the understanding that the body and mind are interconnected.

Reiki: A form of energy healing originating from Japan, involving the transfer of universal energy from the practitioner's palms to the patient to encourage emotional or physical healing.

Resonance: Tesla explored the concept of resonance in his experiments with electromagnetism. Resonance occurs when a system is able to store and easily transfer energy between two or more different storage modes (such as kinetic energy and potential energy in the case of a pendulum). This concept is relevant in energy medicine, where practitioners seek to bring the body's energetic systems into harmonic resonance for healing purposes.

Shamanic Healing: An ancient healing tradition based on the belief that a shaman (spiritual healer) can interact with the spirit world through altered states of consciousness to heal illness or restore balance to the soul.

Subtle Body: A term used in various esoteric traditions to describe a series of psycho-spiritual constituents of living beings, beyond the physical body, including the aura, chakras, and meridians.

Therapeutic Touch: A biofield therapy that involves the practitioner's hands being moved over the patient's body with the intention to detect and modulate imbalances in the patient's energy field.

Tesla Coil: An electrical resonant transformer circuit invented by Tesla. It is capable of producing high-voltage, low-current, high-frequency alternating-current electricity. Tesla coils are used in radio technology, and Tesla envisioned them as a way to wirelessly transmit electrical energy.

Vibrational Medicine: Healing practices are based on the idea that diseases can be diagnosed and treated by applying specific vibrational frequencies to the body, often involving sound, light, or magnetic fields.

Wireless Energy Transmission: Tesla experimented with the wireless transmission of electrical energy, demonstrating the potential to transmit electrical power without wires through the electromagnetic field. This concept of transmitting energy through the air has implications for thinking about the transfer of healing energy in biofield therapies.

Resources for Further Exploration

Books:

- "The Field: The Quest for the Secret Force of the Universe" by Lynne McTaggart
- "Energy Medicine: The Scientific Basis" by James L. Oschman
- "Hands of Light: A Guide to Healing Through the Human Energy Field" by Barbara Brennan

Websites:

- The International Center for Reiki Training (www.reiki.org)
- The Institute of Noetic Sciences (www.noetic.org)
- The Association for Comprehensive Energy Psychology (www.energypsych.org)

Journals:

- "Journal of Alternative and Complementary Medicine"
- "Evidence-Based Complementary and Alternative Medicine"

Conferences:

- Annual International Energy Psychology Conference
- Science and Nonduality Conference

How to Incorporate Energy Practices into Your Life

Daily Meditation and Mindfulness: Start or end your day with a meditation practice that focuses on visualizing or feeling energy flowing through and around your body.

Learn Reiki or Healing Touch: Many communities offer classes that can certify you in basic Reiki or Healing Touch, allowing you to practice these energy-healing techniques on yourself or others.

Practice Yoga or Tai Chi: These ancient practices combine physical movement with breathwork and energy awareness, helping to balance and enhance your body's energy flow.

Engage with Nature: Spend time in natural settings to connect with the Earth's energy. Grounding or earthing, such as walking barefoot on grass, can help realign your energy field with that of the Earth.

Explore Aromatherapy and Crystals: Incorporate essential oils and crystals that resonate with you into your daily routine, as these are believed to carry specific energy frequencies that can influence your biofield.

Seek Out Professional Energy Healers: For personalized guidance, consider consulting with practitioners of energy medicine to address specific health concerns or to deepen your understanding of your energy field.

By incorporating these practices and exploring the suggested resources, you can embark on a journey of self-discovery and healing, embracing the principles of energy medicine to enhance your well-being and connect more deeply with the world around you.

Bibliography

Tesla, Nikola

- Tesla, Nikola. My Inventions: The Autobiography of Nikola Tesla. [Original publication: 1919]
- Seifer, Marc J. Wizard: The Life and Times of Nikola Tesla: Biography of a Genius. Citadel Press, 1998.
- Cheney, Margaret. Tesla: Man Out of Time. Simon & Schuster, 2001.

Energy Medicine & Healing Sciences

- Oschman, James L. Energy Medicine: The Scientific Basis. Elsevier Health Sciences, 2015.
- Oschman, James L. Energy Medicine in Therapeutics and Human Performance. Butterworth-Heinemann, 2003.
- Becker, Robert O., and Selden, Gary. The Body Electric: Electromagnetism and the Foundation of Life. William Morrow Paperbacks, 1998.
- Swanson, Claude. The Synchronized Universe: New Science of the Paranormal. Poseidia Press, 2003.
- Srinivasan, T. M. Energy Medicine and the Human Biofield: A Practical Guide. Partridge Publishing, 2014.

Quantum Physics & Consciousness

- Goswami, Amit. The Quantum Doctor: A Quantum Physicist Explains the Healing Power of Integral Medicine. Hampton Roads Publishing, 2011.

- Radin, Dean. Entangled Minds: Extrasensory Experiences in a Quantum Reality. Paraview Pocket Books, 2006.
- Dispenza, Joe. Becoming Supernatural: How Common People Are Doing the Uncommon. Hay House, 2017.
- Tiller, William A. Conscious Acts of Creation: The Emergence of a New Physics. Pavior, 2001.
- Sheldrake, Rupert. Science and Spiritual Practices: Transformative Experiences and Their Effects on Our Bodies, Brains, and Health. Counterpoint, 2017.

Holistic Healing Practices

- Brennan, Barbara Ann. Light Emerging: The Journey of Personal Healing. Bantam, 1993.
- Eden, Donna, and Feinstein, David. Energy Medicine: Balancing Your Body's Energies for Optimal Health, Joy, and Vitality. TarcherPerigee, 2008.
- Myss, Caroline. Anatomy of the Spirit: The Seven Stages of Power and Healing. Harmony, 1996.
- Dale, Cyndi. The Subtle Body: An Encyclopedia of Your Energetic Anatomy. Sounds True, 2009.
- Gerber, Richard. Vibrational Medicine: The #1 Handbook of Subtle-Energy Therapies. Bear & Company, 2001.
- Bradley, Fiona. Reiki for Life: The Complete Guide to Reiki Practice for Levels 1, 2 & 3. Piatkus, 2016.
- Lipton, Bruce H. The Biology of Belief: Unleashing the Power of Consciousness, Matter & Miracles. Hay House, 2008.

Integrative Medicine & Health Practices

- Weil, Andrew. Spontaneous Healing: How to Discover and Enhance Your Body's Natural

Ability to Maintain and Heal Itself. Ballantine Books, 2000.

- Chopra, Deepak. Quantum Healing: Exploring the Frontiers of Mind/Body Medicine. Bantam, 2015.
- Feinstein, David, and Eden, Donna. The Energies of Love: Invisible Keys to a Fulfilling Partnership. TarcherPerigee, 2014.
- McTaggart, Lynne. The Field: The Quest for the Secret Force of the Universe. HarperCollins, 2008.

Biophysics & Electromagnetism

- Polk, C., and Postow, E. (Eds.). Handbook of Biological Effects of Electromagnetic Fields. CRC Press, 1995.
- BioInitiative Report: A Rationale for a Biologically-based Public Exposure Standard for Electromagnetic Fields (ELF and RF). Available at www.bioinitiative.org.

Energy Healing Modalities

- Miles, Patricia. Reiki: A Comprehensive Guide. TarcherPerigee, 2008.
- Hover-Kramer, Dorothea. Healing Touch: A Guidebook for Practitioners. Delmar Cengage Learning, 2002.
- Kreiger, Dolores. The Therapeutic Touch: How to Use Your Hands to Help or to Heal. Prentice Hall, 1979.

Journals & Periodicals

- The Journal of Alternative and Complementary Medicine
- Evidence-Based Complementary and Alternative Medicine
- Global Advances in Health and Medicine
- Journal of Bodywork and Movement Therapies

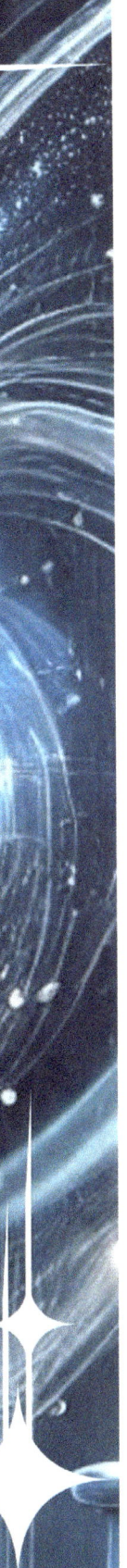

Online Resources

- The Tesla Science Foundation: www.teslasciencefoundation.org
- The Institute of Noetic Sciences (IONS): www.noetic.org
- The HeartMath Institute: www.heartmath.org
- The International Society for the Study of Subtle Energies and Energy Medicine (ISSSEEM): www.issseem.org

Acknowledgments

First and foremost, I extend my deepest gratitude to Nikola Tesla, whose visionary genius continues to illuminate new paths in science and healing. Tesla's work transcends time, and his groundbreaking ideas on energy and electromagnetism have inspired this book and the ongoing exploration of energy medicine. His dream of harnessing the unseen forces of nature for the betterment of humanity lives on, and it is in the spirit of his legacy that this work continues.

I also wish to express my immense appreciation to the researchers, scientists, and practitioners who are advancing the field of energy medicine. Your tireless dedication to exploring the frontiers of human health, consciousness, and energy healing has been an invaluable resource. Without your contributions, the bridges between science and healing would remain incomplete. This book is built upon your discoveries and insights, and I am honored to share your pioneering work.

A special thanks to my mentors, colleagues, and collaborators—your guidance, wisdom, and support have been instrumental in navigating the complexities of merging Tesla's visionary ideas with today's scientific advancements. I deeply value the input of those who have worked at the intersection of energy, healing, and consciousness, and your influence can be felt throughout the pages of this book.

To the members of the Tesla Science Foundation, The Institute of Noetic Sciences, and other like-minded organizations, thank you for continuing to preserve, expand, and explore Tesla's legacy in innovative and forward-thinking ways. Your dedication to the intersection of science and spirituality provides a rich foundation for the work we are all collectively contributing to the future of healing.

My heartfelt thanks also go to the editorial team, whose keen eyes and thoughtful input have been vital to the completion of this manuscript. Your patience, insight, and dedication throughout the editing process have made this book a stronger and more focused work. I am deeply grateful for your efforts.

To my family and friends, your unwavering support throughout the writing of this book has been an anchor. Your belief in my vision has carried me through the challenges and has provided the encouragement needed to complete this project. Thank you for your understanding and for being a source of constant strength.

To the readers of *Beyond Tesla: Advancing the Science of Energy Healing*, I hope you find within these pages not only an exploration of Tesla's continuing influence but also a spark of curiosity that drives you to look deeper into the connections between energy, health, and human potential. May this book serve as a tool for your personal and professional growth, inspiring new ideas and applications in the field of energy medicine.

Lastly, to the universe and the infinite energy that connects us all—thank you for the mysteries that continue to unfold and for the subtle forces that remind us there is so much more to discover. It is through this interconnectedness that we continue to evolve and heal, both individually and collectively.

This book is the result of many hands, minds, and hearts coming together. Together, we move forward, advancing the science of energy healing and creating new possibilities for the future of health and wellness.

Thank you all.

Dr. Constance Santego

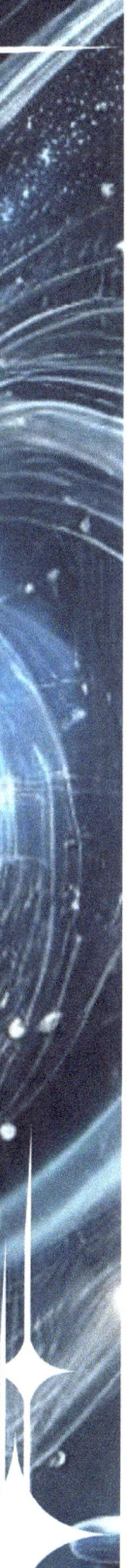

Message from the Author

Dear Readers,

From the depths of my heart and the heights of my imagination, *Beyond Tesla: Advancing the Science of Energy Healing* is a continuation of the journey we began together with *Tesla and the Future of Energy Medicine*. What began as a vision—a dream to bring holistic and energy medicine into the esteemed halls of modern healthcare—has now evolved into a deeper exploration of the science, philosophy, and innovation that is shaping the future of healing.

As I reflect on this journey, I am reminded that the greatest breakthroughs in medicine often come from challenging the status quo and from daring to believe in what lies beyond the known. Nikola Tesla, whose brilliance continues to inspire this work, envisioned a world where energy, frequency, and vibration would be harnessed for the betterment of humanity. In this book, we take that vision further, exploring how Tesla's ideas have inspired cutting-edge advancements in energy medicine that blend ancient wisdom with modern science.

My goal with *Beyond Tesla* is not just to present theories but to challenge perceptions and inspire a shift in how we view energy medicine—not as an alternative or fringe practice but as an integral part of healthcare's future. I imagine a world where energy healing is as respected and scientifically grounded as any other medical discipline, where its potential is fully realized, and its practitioners recognized for their contributions to health and well-being.

Writing this book has been a journey of balancing the visionary with the empirical, the imaginative with the evidence-based. Like Tesla, I have walked the line between the creative and the scientific, seeking to bridge the gap between holistic medicine and rigorous scientific inquiry. This book reflects that balance, offering both the advanced concepts of energy healing and practical applications grounded in the latest research.

Looking forward, I envision the establishment of a Tesla Institute of Energy Medicine, a place where the pioneering work of Tesla and the advancements in energy healing can come together in a center of learning, research, and practice. Having once led an accredited college where holistic modalities were taught, I now aspire to elevate energy medicine to even greater heights of credibility and impact.

To the visionaries, scientists, healers, and practitioners who have dedicated themselves to the advancement of energy medicine—thank you. Your work is the foundation upon which this book stands, and your courage in exploring new frontiers continues to inspire me. Together, we are shaping a future where energy medicine takes its rightful place alongside the most respected fields of healthcare.

I invite you, dear readers, to join me beyond these pages. Let's continue this journey together through workshops, discussions, and a growing community of like-minded individuals dedicated to the future of energy healing. On my website and through social media, we can explore these concepts further,

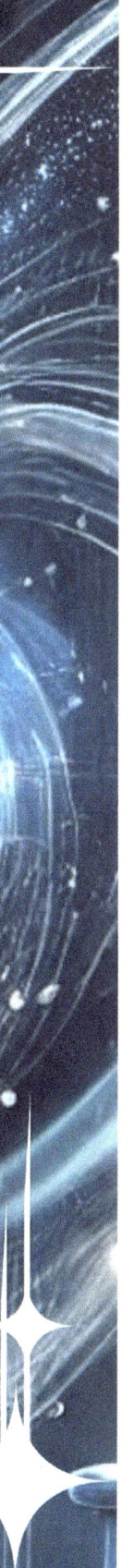

advancing toward a future where the full potential of energy medicine is realized.

This book is a stepping stone in our shared path—a path inspired by the legacy of Nikola Tesla and driven by the collective desire to explore the infinite possibilities of energy healing.

With deepest gratitude and optimism for what lies ahead,
Dr. Constance Santego

About the Author

Dr. Constance Santego stands at the crossroads of science, wellness, and spirituality, guiding individuals on their journey toward holistic health and self-transformation. With a lifelong passion for integrating ancient wisdom and modern scientific advancements, Dr. Santego has become a beacon in the field of natural medicine, offering tools and insights that foster healing, growth, and personal evolution.

With a doctorate in Natural Medicine and a rich background that spans a wide array of healing modalities—ranging from Reiki Master and Educator to Life Coach and Spiritual Guide—Dr. Santego's expertise is vast. Her dedication to helping others unlock their potential is reflected in her diverse roles, each of which is driven by her commitment to holistic well-being and self-empowerment. Her work emphasizes the interconnectedness of mind, body, and spirit, encouraging individuals to embrace their wholeness and to live in alignment with their highest selves.

An accomplished author, Dr. Santego has written extensively on topics of energy, healing, love, and personal fulfillment, blending traditional knowledge with forward-thinking insights. Her books serve as both practical guides and spiritual roadmaps, offering readers transformative tools to enhance their lives through self-awareness, healing, and inner growth.

Through her teachings and writings, Dr. Santego invites others to embark on a personal journey of discovery, one where the physical and metaphysical realms converge to illuminate the path forward. Her holistic approach inspires individuals to transcend their limitations, tap into their innate power, and create meaningful, fulfilling lives.

In addition to her literary contributions, Dr. Santego is the founder of a holistic health and wellness school, a transformative space that empowers students to explore their healing potential and share their knowledge with the world. Her school is a crucible for personal transformation, equipping students with the tools they need to heal themselves and others.

In *Beyond Tesla: Advancing the Science of Energy Healing*, Dr. Santego takes readers deeper into the intersections of Nikola Tesla's pioneering energy theories and the evolving world of energy medicine. This work, co-authored with ChatGPT, represents a visionary leap forward, blending human creativity with artificial intelligence to explore the profound possibilities that emerge when past wisdom meets future innovations in healing.

To learn more about Dr. Constance Santego's teachings, explore her works, or join her in the transformative journey of holistic healing, visit www.constancesantego.ca. There, the fusion of wisdom, healing, and empowerment awaits.

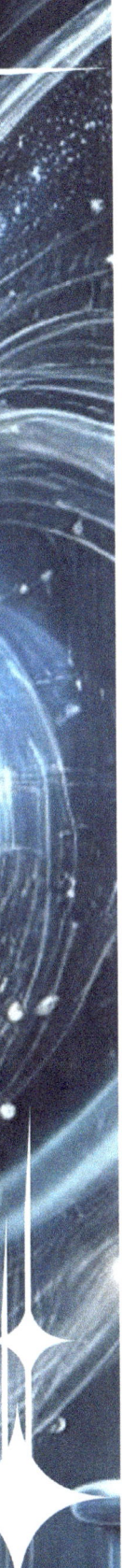

Discover More

Embark on an Adventure with "Ikona – Discover Your Inner Genie"

Dive deeper into the world of empowerment and self-discovery with a range of offerings designed to inspire and transform. Explore the full spectrum of Constance Santego's motivational products, personalized coaching sessions, spiritual retreats, engaging live events, and enriching educational programs.

Connect, Learn, and Grow:

- Website: Journey further into our resources and offerings at www.ConstanceSantego.ca.
- Instagram: Join our community @Constance_Santego for daily inspiration and insights.
- Facebook: Stay updated with the latest events and connect with like-minded individuals on Constance Santego's Facebook Page.
- YouTube: Subscribe to Constance Santego's YouTube Channel for free resources, meditations, and more to guide you on your path to self-improvement.

Your journey toward personal growth and enlightenment is just a click away. Discover the tools and support you need to unlock your potential and manifest your dreams.

"Everything is Energy, and that is all there is to it. Match the frequency of the reality you want, and you cannot help but get that reality. It can be no other way. It is not philosophyIt is Physics."
—Albert Einstein

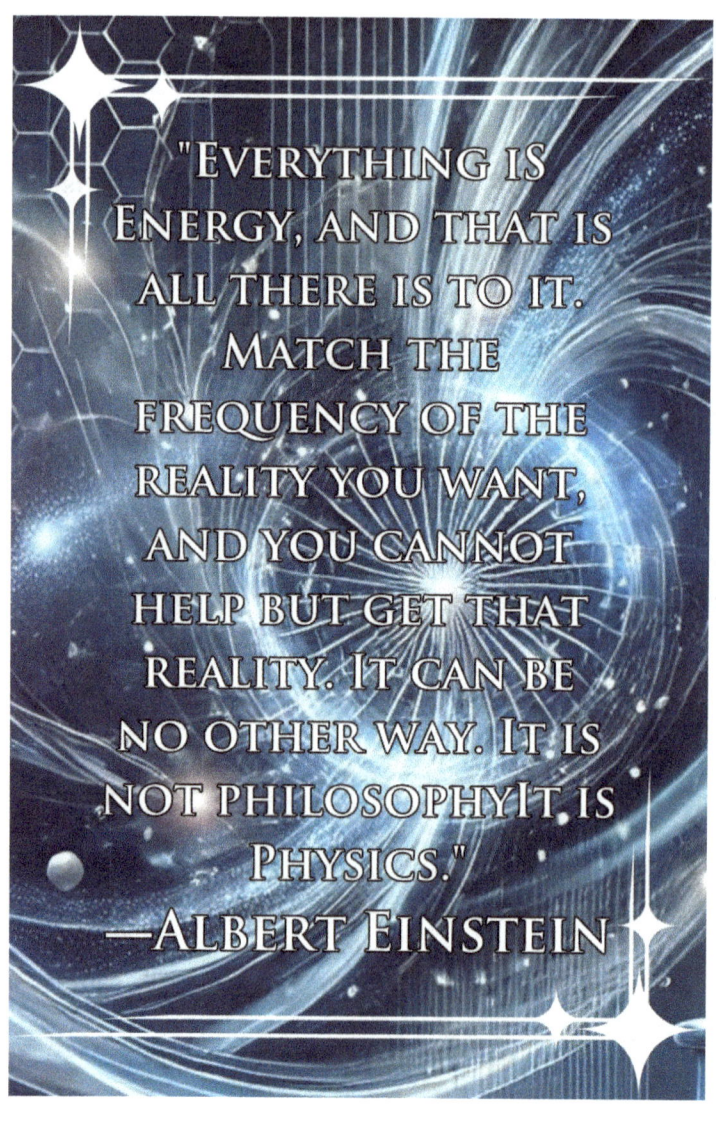

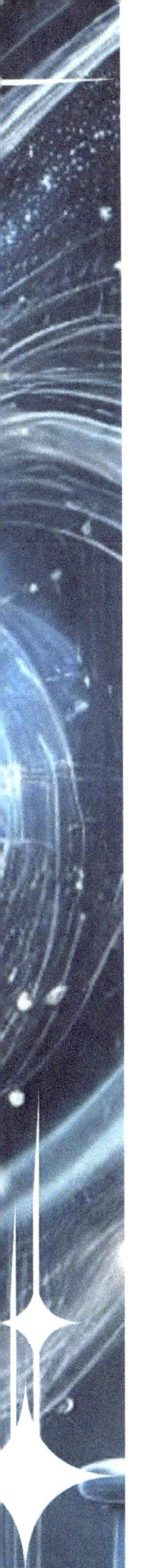

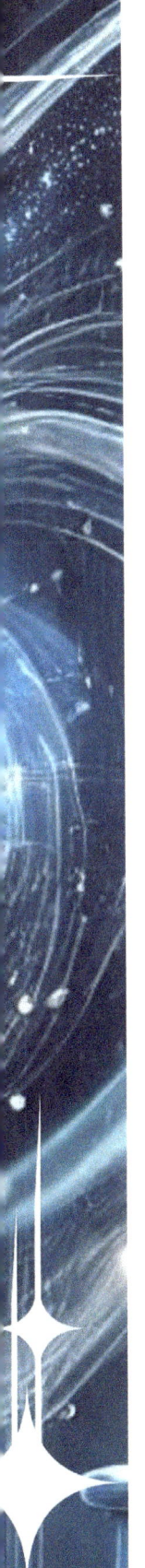

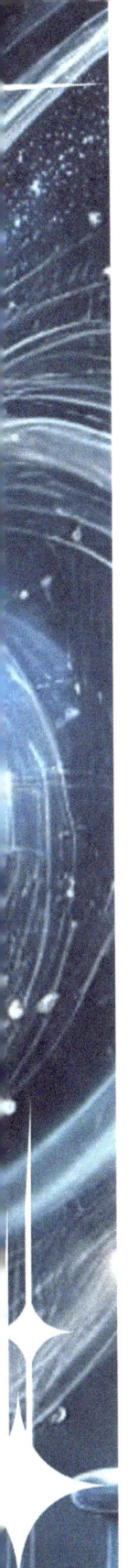

www.ingramcontent.com/pod-product-compliance
Lightning Source LLC
Chambersburg PA
CBHW071014120626
46546CB00003B/1079